THE GREEN LANTERN CHRONICLES

VOLUME THREE

ALL STORIES WRITTEN BY **JOHN BROOME** AND ART PENCILLED BY **GIL KANE** AND
INKED BY **JOE GIELLA**, UNLESS OTHERWISE NOTED.

Julius Schwartz – EDITOR-ORIGINAL SERIES ☆ Bob Harras – GROUP EDITOR-COLLECTED EDITIONS
Bob Joy – EDITOR ☆ Robbin Brosterman – DESIGN DIRECTOR-BOOKS

DC COMICS

Diane Nelson - PRESIDENT ☆ Dan DiDio and Jim Lee - CO-PUBLISHERS
Geoff Johns - CHIEF CREATIVE OFFICER ☆ Patrick Caldon - EVP-FINANCE AND ADMINISTRATION
John Rood - EVP-SALES, MARKETING AND BUSINESS DEVELOPMENT ☆ Amy Genkins - SVP-BUSINESS AND LEGAL AFFAIRS
Steve Rotterdam - SVP-SALES AND MARKETING ☆ John Cunningham - VP-MARKETING ☆ Terri Cunningham - VP-MANAGING EDITOR
Alison Gill - VP-MANUFACTURING ☆ David Hyde - VP-PUBLICITY ☆ Sue Pohja - VP-BOOK TRADE SALES
Alysse Soll - VP-ADVERTISING AND CUSTOM PUBLISHING ☆ Bob Wayne - VP-SALES ☆ Mark Chiarello - ART DIRECTOR

ISBN: 978-1-4012-2915-3
Printed by Quad/Graphics, Dubuque, IA, USA 9/13/10

Cover art by: Carmine Infantino and Joe Giella

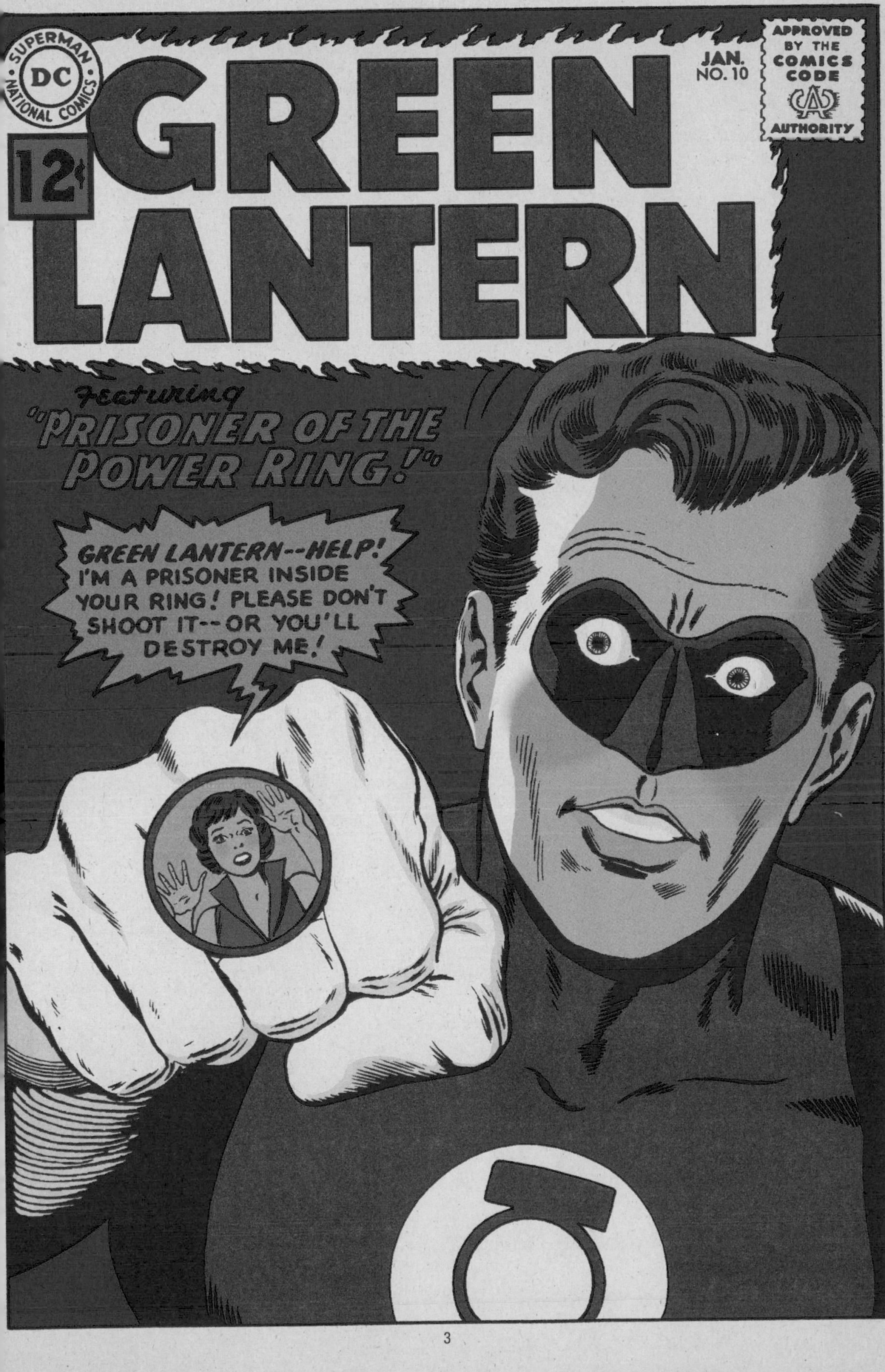
SUPERMAN DC NATIONAL COMICS
12¢
GREEN LANTERN
JAN. NO. 10
APPROVED BY THE COMICS CODE AUTHORITY
Featuring "PRISONER OF THE POWER RING!"
GREEN LANTERN--HELP! I'M A PRISONER INSIDE YOUR RING! PLEASE DON'T SHOOT IT--OR YOU'LL DESTROY ME!

GREEN LANTERN

...AND IT IS *YOUR BEAM, GREEN LANTERN*--OPERATING THROUGH *ME*, YOUR *POWER RING*--THAT HAS ENDANGERED THE HUMANS IN THE *ATOM WORLD!*

THEY'RE DOOMED-- UNLESS I CAN FIND A WAY TO SAVE THEM!

DR. BLANDING, A BRILLIANT PHYSICIST, CONCEIVED THE IDEA OF ESCAPING FROM THIS WORLD OF WORRY AND THREAT OF WAR, BY FLEEING INTO AN *ATOM WORLD!*
BUT THERE, AS IT HAPPENS, THE SCIENTIST AND HIS PARTY MET MORE DANGER THAN THEY COULD EVER HAVE IMAGINED!
DANGER FROM WHICH ONLY *GREEN LANTERN* COULD SAVE THEM--AS, BY A FLUKE OF FATE, IT WAS *ONLY* HE WHO COULD HAVE CAUSED THEIR PERIL!

PRISONER OF THE POWER RING!

CRACK TEST PILOT HAL JORDAN (ALIAS GREEN LANTERN) PUTS A NEW PLANE THROUGH ITS PACES...

THE WINGS STAND UP FINE UNDER A 15-G STRESS! THIS BABY CAN REALLY GO!

NOW TO TRY OUT HER RATE-OF-CLIMB AND PERFORMANCE AT HIGH ALTITUDE...

AFTER THE CRAFT HAS MET ALL TESTS, HIGH IN THE STRATOSPHERE...

EH? WE CHOSE THIS TEST AREA BECAUSE NO MILITARY OR COMMERCIAL PLANES FLY THROUGH HERE! WHERE IS THAT JET GOING?

AS A BANKING MANEUVER CARRIES HAL INTO POSITION FOR A BETTER VIEW OF HIS SURPRISE VISITOR...

THAT'S STRANGE! NO MARKINGS ON THAT BIRD...WAIT A SECOND! I JUST REMEMBERED SOMETHING! WHAT WAS THAT GOVERNMENT CIRCULAR PIEFACE CALLED TO MY ATTENTION YESTERDAY MORNING?

IN HIS MIND'S EYE HAL SEES HIS LITTLE ESKIMO GREASE MONKEY BEFORE HIM, AND HEARS HIM SPEAK...

...SMUGGLERS SNEAKING VALUABLE DIAMONDS INTO THIS COUNTRY! WASHINGTON SUSPECTS THAT AN AIRPLANE IS BEING USED TO SLIP PAST OUR CUSTOMS GUARDS! ALL AIRFIELDS ARE BEING ALERTED, HAL...

...AND ALL PILOTS ARE ASKED TO BE ON THE LOOKOUT FOR ANY FAST-MOVING UNIDENTIFIED CRAFT!

FAST-MOVING... UNIDENTIFIED... THIS ONE SEEMS TO FIT THE BILL!

2.

WITH QUIET DECISION, THE ACE FLYER POINTS HIS PLANE AFTER THE DIS-APPEARING JET...

THAT BIRD CAN GO... BUT THIS BABY UNDER ME IS SO FAST, I'LL HAVE **NO TROUBLE** KEEPING IT IN VIEW! GOT TO FIND OUT **WHERE** IT'S HEADING..!

AND SOON, MAINTAINING ALTITUDE TO AVOID ALARMING HIS QUARRY, HAL SEES...

LANDING ON WHAT LOOKS LIKE A DRIED-OUT LAKE IN THE MIDDLE OF THESE MOUNTAINS!? WELL, IF IT CAN GO DOWN, **SO CAN I**!

AS THE INTREPID ACE CARRIES OUT HIS OBJECTIVE EXPERTLY...

I'M LANDING ON A CORNER OF THE LAKE OUT OF SIGHT OF THE OTHER PLANE! I DON'T WANT THEM TO SEE ME UNTIL I'M READY...

666

AND MOMENTS LATER...

SOMETHING TELLS ME I'M ABOUT TO CATCH A CREW OF **DIAMOND SMUGGLERS** RED-HANDED! OR RATHER-- THAT **GREEN LANTERN** IS ABOUT TO! THERE WOULD BE **NO HONEST REASON** FOR THAT PLANE TO COME DOWN HERE!

BUT, THEN, AS THE EMERALD CRUSADER IS ABOUT TO USE HIS MIGHTY POWER BEAM TO CATAPULT OFF...

DON'T USE YOUR RING!

GREAT GUARDIANS! THAT TELEPATHIC VOICE! IT'S COMING FROM--

GREEN LANTERN! PLEASE DON'T USE YOUR RING --OR YOU'LL DESTROY ME!

A GIRL INSIDE MY RING!?

③

6

YOU-- UHH...

SHE--SHE SEEMS TO HAVE *FAINTED!* BUT WHAT DID SHE MEAN--I MUSTN'T USE MY RING OR I WOULD *DESTROY* HER?

IN HIS PERPLEXITY, THE MIND OF THE GREEN-CLAD CRUSADER WORKS SWIFTLY...

I'VE STILL GOT TO CATCH THOSE SMUGGLERS, BUT NOW I DON'T DARE USE MY RING! MY BEST BET IS TO GO AFTER THE CROOKS WITH MY BARE HANDS, AND THEN... AFTERWARDS...

...TRY TO FIND OUT *WHO* THE GIRL IS AND HOW IN THE WORLD SHE GOT *INTO* MY RING! MAYBE WHEN SHE REVIVES SHE'LL BE ABLE TO TELL ME! I SURE HOPE SO!

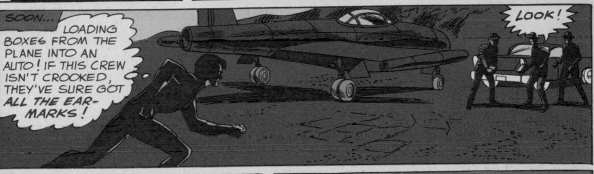

SOON... LOADING BOXES FROM THE PLANE INTO AN AUTO! IF THIS CREW ISN'T CROOKED, THEY'VE SURE GOT *ALL THE EAR-MARKS!*

LOOK!

GREEN LANTERN!?

DRAWING GUNS! GOT TO GET INTO CLOSE QUARTERS WITH THEM FAST-- MAKE IT HARD FOR THEM TO USE THEIR WEAPONS!

WITH DEVASTATING EFFECT, A GREEN-STREAKED METEOR ERUPTS AMONG THE WOULD-BE KILLERS...

I'M GETTING OUT OF HERE!

7

As **GL's** IRON-HARD FISTS ACCOUNT FOR THE SECOND MEMBER OF THE GANG...

THE THIRD ONE GETTING INTO THE CAR! GOT TO STOP HIM!

THEN... GREAT SCOTT! IN THE HEAT OF ACTION I FLASHED A BIT OF POWER FROM MY RING! I HOPE THAT GIRL ISN'T HARMED! BUT NO TIME TO FIND OUT NOW--!

BUNDLING HIS TWO UNCONSCIOUS CAPTIVES INTO THEIR PLANE, THE EMERALD WARRIOR STARTS UP THE ENGINE AND MOMENTS LATER...

I'VE GOT TO STOP THAT RUNAWAY SMUGGLER! AND FORTUNATELY I CAN FLY THIS JET-- OR **ANY** JET FOR THAT MATTER!

THE NEXT MOMENT...

THAT'LL STOP HIS GETAWAY!

VOOMP!

I DON'T THINK THAT CRASH INJURED THE CROOK AT THE WHEEL! NOW TO LAND AND ADD THAT DRIVER TO MY COLLECTION!

AND SHORTLY, WITH ALL THREE OF THE GANG MADE HELPLESS AND STOWED SAFELY IN THE JET, *GREEN LANTERN* USES HIS OWN PLANE RADIO TO CONTACT NEARBY POLICE...

...AND YOU'LL FIND THE GANG IN THEIR PLANE TIED UP! I'VE GIVEN YOU THE *MAP COORDINATES* OF THIS SPOT, SO YOU CAN'T MISS IT!

WE'LL BE THERE IN AN HOUR, *GREEN LANTERN!* THANKS!

WELL, THAT TAKES CARE OF THOSE SMUGGLERS! NOW TO FIND OUT ABOUT THAT GIRL IN MY RING!

SHE--SHE'S GONE! I COULDN'T HAVE DREAMED SHE WAS THERE! I SAW HER--SHE SPOKE TO ME! BUT WHERE IS SHE NOW?

AS THE GLADIATOR PUZZLES OVER THE STRANGE PROBLEM...

I CAN'T SEEM TO GET THAT GIRL OFF MY MIND! DID THAT BURST OF GREEN BEAM I ACCIDENTALLY SHOT OUT DESTROY HER? WHERE DID SHE COME FROM? HOW DID SHE GET INTO MY RING? I'VE *GOT* TO FIND OUT!

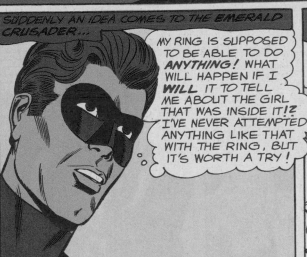

SUDDENLY AN IDEA COMES TO THE *EMERALD CRUSADER*...

MY RING IS SUPPOSED TO BE ABLE TO DO *ANYTHING!* WHAT WILL HAPPEN IF I *WILL* IT TO TELL ME ABOUT THE GIRL THAT WAS INSIDE IT!? I'VE NEVER ATTEMPTED ANYTHING LIKE THAT WITH THE RING, BUT IT'S WORTH A TRY!

OUT OF THE VIGOROUS GREEN-CLAD HERO POURS A POWERFUL THOUGHT IMPULSE...

POWER RING, TELL ME ABOUT THE GIRL! I WANT TO KNOW ALL ABOUT HER!

WILL THIS WORK? WILL THE RING BE ABLE TO REPLY--?

6.

THEN, AS GL'S HEART BOUNDS JOYOUSLY...

THE RING IS BEGINNING TO ANSWER ME--!

...HER NAME IS BEVERLY BLANDING!... I CAN TELL YOU ABOUT HER... BECAUSE DURING THE TIME SHE WAS INSIDE ME... I ABSORBED THE EMANATIONS FROM HER BRAIN!

BUT IN ORDER TO DESCRIBE... HOW SHE CAME TO BE INSIDE ME... I MUST FIRST TELL YOU ABOUT HER FATHER, DR. JASON BLANDING, THE PHYSICIST! EIGHT MONTHS AGO IN THEIR HOME IN THE WEST...

"...DR. BLANDING CAME ACROSS A REMARKABLE DISCOVERY..."

THIS NEW **MESON RADIATION** I'VE DEVELOPED HAS THE AMAZING ABILITY TO SHRINK LIVING CREATURES DOWN TO IN-FINITESIMAL SIZE-- WITHOUT HARMING THEM!

"AS THE BRILLIANT SCIENTIST PORED OVER HIS DISCOVERY."

NO DOUBT OF IT! BY MY CAL-CULATIONS, THE CAT LANDED UNHURT IN AN ATOMIC WORLD-- A WORLD MUCH LIKE OURS, BUT **INSIDE THE ATOM!** AND **THAT** GIVES ME AN IDEA...!

"LATER, DR. BLANDING BROACHED A STARTLING PROPOSAL TO HIS FAMILY, HIS WIFE AND DAUGHTER BEVERLY..."

...YOU BOTH KNOW THAT FOR YEARS I'VE DREAMED OF GETTING AWAY FROM THIS LIFE WHERE WAR AND CONFLICT ALWAYS THREATEN US! NOW WE HAVE AN OPPORTUNITY! WE CAN GO INTO THE **ATOMIC WORLD**--TO LIVE THE REST OF OUR YEARS IN PEACE AND CONTENTMENT! WILL YOU TWO COME WITH ME?

"MRS. BLANDING AND BEVERLY AGREED! BUT THERE WAS A HITCH, IN THE PERSON OF WILL CHAMBERS, BEVERLY'S BOY FRIEND..."

I CAN'T LET YOU TAKE BEV AWAY FROM ME, DR. BLANDING! I LOVE HER--I CAN'T BEAR TO LOSE HER!

IN THAT CASE, MY BOY, THE ANSWER IS SIMPLE! YOU CAN COME WITH US!

7

AND SO IT WAS ARRANGED! BUT WHEN THE TIME CAME FOR THE DRAMATIC DEPARTURE, DR. BLANDING HAD ONE FINAL WORD...

I KNOW OF NO WAY TO REVERSE THE PROCESS! SO THERE MAY BE NO RETURN FOR US! IF ANY OF YOU WANTS TO CHANGE HIS OR HER MIND--NOW IS THE TIME TO SPEAK UP--BEFORE I PULL THIS LEVER!

NO ONE SPOKE! DR. BLANDING'S HAND CLOSED ON THE LEVER, GRIMLY, DETERMINEDLY! HE PULLED IT...

"WHAT HAPPENED NEXT WAS ALMOST INSTANTANEOUS! A FLOOD OF QUEER BRILLIANT LIGHT FILLED THE ROOM! THE FOUR PEOPLE FELT THEMSELVES GRIPPED BY AN INCREDIBLE FORCE, THAT AFFECTED EVEN THE CLOTHES THEY WORE..."

WE'RE SHRINKING!

EVERYTHING AROUND US HAS BECOME HUGE!

WILL WE GET THERE? WILL THE MESON APPARATUS SEND US INTO THE UTOPIAN ATOMIC WORLD FORECAST BY MY CALCULATIONS? IT HAS TO! IT HAS TO!

PRISONER OF THE POWER RING! PART TWO

"AND WHEN THE MIST DISSOLVED FROM BEFORE THE EYES OF THE ADVENTUROUS FOURSOME..."

WE'RE SAFE! THANK GOODNESS!

SO THIS IS IT-- THE ATOMIC WORLD PREDICTED BY MY EQUATIONS! LISTEN, EVERYONE...

FROM NOW ON WE WILL PROCEED TO CONSTRUCT A *SCIENTIFIC UTOPIA* WHERE ALL OF US --AND ULTIMATELY OUR DESCENDANTS --WILL LIVE IN PEACE AND HARMONY!

"AND INDEED WITHIN SIX MONTHS DR. BLANDING'S DREAM SEEMED IN A FAIR WAY TOWARD COMPLETE FULFILLMENT..."

IT'S AMAZING WHAT YOU'VE DONE HERE IN A MATTER OF MONTHS, SIR! NOT ONLY DO WE HAVE SHELTER AND A GOOD FOOD SUPPLY--BUT YOU'VE BUILT THOSE *ROBOTS* WHICH ARE NOW CARRYING ON MOST OF THE WORK!

COMING HERE GAVE ME A BURST OF *CREATIVE ENERGY*, WILL! BUT YOU AND BEVERLY HAVE HELPED ME A LOT-- LET'S NOT FORGET THAT!

"THE ROBOTS--POWERED BY INTERNAL ATOMIC MOTORS BUILT BY DR. BLANDING --WERE THE SCIENTIST'S PRIZE CREATIONS..."

YOUR ROBOTS DO EVERYTHING FOR US, DAD! THERE'S HARDLY ANYTHING LEFT FOR US TO DO!

THAT IS A SCIENTIFIC UTOPIA, MY DEAR! ARE YOU COMPLAINING?

"BEVERLY WASN'T EXACTLY COMPLAINING, BUT SHE AND WILL DID HAVE CERTAIN RESERVATIONS.."

I KNOW DAD MEANS WHAT'S BEST FOR US, WILL, BUT I CAN'T HELP FEELING HE'S LETTING THE ROBOTS DO *TOO MUCH*! AND NOW HE'S EVEN *ARMED* SOME OF THEM WITH WEAPONS THAT HE'S MADE!

I'VE BEEN WORRIED ABOUT THAT TOO, BEV...

YOUR DAD FEELS WE'VE NEVER EXPLORED THIS ATOMIC WORLD COMPLETELY-- AND THERE **MAY** BE ENEMIES HERE TO THREATEN US! HE SAYS THE ROBOTS WILL PROTECT US!

YES... BUT IT STILL MAKES ME UNCOMFORTABLE TO SEE THEM WITH WEAPONS!

"IT WAS SOON AFTER THAT THE STRANGE THINGS BEGAN TO HAPPEN..."

THAT'S ODD! THE ROBOTS SEEM TO BE **FIGHTING** AMONG THEMSELVES !?

"THE NEXT MOMENT..."

GOOD GOSH! ONE OF THE QUARRELING ROBOTS HAS **SHOT THE OTHER ONE!**

"LATER, A GRIM QUARTET OF HUMANS HELD A COUNCIL PRESIDED OVER BY THE SCIENTIST..."

SOMETHING IS TERRIBLY WRONG WITH OUR ROBOTS! BUT I THINK I'VE TRACED THE TROUBLE! FROM SOMEWHERE --PROBABLY FROM THE WORLD WE LEFT BEHIND ...

"A TRICKLE OF MYSTERIOUS **GREEN RADIATION** IS FILTERING DOWN INTO OUR ATOMIC WORLD! SO FAR IT HAS NO EFFECT ON **US** -- BUT IT IS DERANGING THE MECHANISM OF THE ROBOTS! OUR ENTIRE EXISTENCE HERE IS IN DANGER!

THERE'S NO TELLING WHAT THE ROBOTS WILL DO NEXT! AND WE MAY NOT BE ABLE TO STOP THEM! THERE'S ONLY ONE WAY TO SAVE OURSELVES! WE MUST FIND OUT THE **SOURCE** OF THE **GREEN ENERGY**-- AND CUT IT OFF AT ALL COSTS!

"DR. BLANDING WORKED WITH FEVERISH HASTE, AND SOON..."

THERE'S NO TIME TO EXPLAIN MY NEW MACHINE TO YOU, BEVERLY! ALL I CAN TELL YOU IS THIS: IT SHOULD *PROJECT ME BODILY* BACK ALONG THE PATH OF THE INCOMING MYSTERY RAYS, SO THAT I CAN FIND OUT WHERE THEY'RE COMING FROM!

I DON'T WANT TO WORRY THE OTHERS! OF COURSE, THIS ATTEMPT IS DANGEROUS! BUT I'M DETERMINED TO TRY IT!

STAND BACK-- I'M GOING TO WALK UNDER THE RADIATION BEAM!

"BUT THEN..."

NO, FATHER! YOU'RE TOO VALUABLE HERE! IF ANYONE MAKES THIS DANGEROUS ATTEMPT TO SAVE US--LET IT BE ME!

BEVERLY! WHAT--?

"AND THE NEXT MOMENT..."

BEVERLY! SHE STEPPED UNDER THE RADIATION-BEAM! SHE'S BEGINNING TO *DISAPPEAR!*

"DR. BLANDING'S DEVICE WORKED PERFECTLY! IT PROJECTED BEVERLY BACK ALONG THE 'MYSTERIOUS GREEN ENERGY' UNTIL FINALLY SHE CAME TO REST... INSIDE ME!!"

PLEASE DON'T USE YOUR RING-- OR YOU'LL *DESTROY* ME!!

GREAT GUARDIANS! THEN-- WHAT HAPPENED TO THE GIRL? WHERE IS SHE?

WHEN YOU FIRED OFF THAT TINY SPURT OF POWER FROM YOUR RING A WHILE AGO IT CATAPULTED HER BACK TO HER FATHER'S LABORATORY! SHE'S UNCONSCIOUS-- BUT NOT FATALLY HURT!

GRIMLY, GREEN LANTERN MAKES UP HIS MIND ON THE INSTANT...

I'VE GOT TO MAKE SURE SHE'S ALL RIGHT! AND THE ONLY WAY TO DO THAT IS TO USE MY *POWER BEAM* TO GO DOWN INTO THE *ATOMIC WORLD* MYSELF!

POWERED BY HIS ALL-POWERFUL EMERALD RAY, HE IS SOON ON HIS WAY TOWARD HIS OBJECTIVE...

DR. BLANDING NEEDED A *MESON APPARATUS* TO REACH THE ATOM WORLD, BUT I CAN DO THE SAME THING MORE SIMPLY WITH MY RING! THE ATOMS OF EARTH AROUND ME NOW ARE HUGE...

MEANWHILE... BEVERLY, ARE YOU ALL RIGHT?

IT WAS MOSTLY *SHOCK* THAT MADE ME LOSE CONSCIOUSNESS, DAD! BUT I'M FEELING BETTER!

AS THE YOUNG GIRL REVEALS HER DISCOVERY...

THEN IT WAS THE BEAM FROM *GREEN LANTERN'S* RING--FILTERING DOWN HERE--WHICH CAUSED OUR ROBOTS TO RUN AMUCK?

YES! BUT--WHAT'S THAT!?

DARTING OUT-OF-DOORS, THEY VIEW A FEARSOME SIGHT...

THE ROBOTS--THEY'VE DIVIDED INTO TWO GROUPS-- TWO *ARMIES*--AND ARE MAKING WAR ON EACH OTHER!?

YES! BUT I HAVEN'T TOLD ANY-ONE THE WORST YET! A DEADLY RADIATION IS BUILD-ING UP IN EACH ROBOT! THEY'RE COMPLETELY OUT OF CONTROL! AND WHEN THE RADIATION REACHES A CERTAIN POINT THEY'LL EXPLODE--WITH ATOMIC FORCE--AND BLOW UP THIS WORLD!

12

BUT AT THE SAME TIME *GREEN LANTERN*, LANDING IN THE ATOMIC WORLD, HAS REACHED THE SAME CONCLUSIONS!

ACCORDING TO WHAT MY RING HAS DETECTED, EACH OF THESE ROBOTS IS ON THE VERGE OF *EXPLODING* !! I'VE GOT TO SAVE DR. BLANDING AND THE OTHER HUMANS HERE FROM BEING DESTROYED!

AT ONCE THE GREEN-CLAD CHAMPION PLUNGES INTO ACTION...

MY ONLY CHANCE IS TO DESTROY THESE WARRING ROBOTS AS FAST AS POSSIBLE! THERE GOES ONE ...!

...AND ANOTHER!

THAT HUMAN--IS OUR ENEMY! WE MUST FIGHT HIM--

EH? NOW THEY'VE SUDDENLY STOPPED FIGHTING AMONG THEMSELVES--AND TURNED ON ME! BULLETS--MISSILES-- FLYING AT ME FROM EVERY SIDE!

ZIIP!

VIIP!

ZIIP!

IN HIS CRISIS OF PERIL, *GREEN LANTERN* POURS EVERY OUNCE OF WILLPOWER BEHIND HIS MARVELOUS RING FOR A DIE-- HARD EFFORT...

MY RING IS RETURNING THE DEADLY GUNFIRE AIMED AT ME--SHOOTING IT BACK AT THE ROBOTS WITH EVEN GREATER SPEED THAN IT CAME FROM THEM!

WHAAP!

ZIING!

ZZZIIIP!

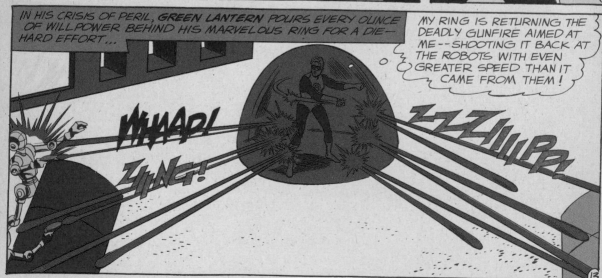

13

16

WHEN THE FURIOUS BATTLE ENDS...

FINISHED THEM! BUT NOW TO SEE IF DR. BLANDING AND THE OTHERS ARE ALL RIGHT...

AS *GL* DISCOVERS THAT HIS FELLOW HUMANS SURVIVED THE "ROBOT WAR"...

IT WAS WONDERFUL OF YOU TO COME DOWN HERE AND TRY TO HELP US, *GREEN LANTERN!* BUT I'M AFRAID THAT ALL YOUR EFFORTS HAVE BEEN *WASTED!*

WASTED? WHAT DO YOU MEAN, DR. BLANDING?

MY INSTRUMENTS SHOW THAT EVEN THOUGH YOU KNOCKED THE ROBOTS OUT AND DESTROYED THEM, THE DEADLY RADIATION THAT WAS STARTED IN THEM IS *STILL MOUNTING!* NOTHING CAN HELP US! IN A FEW MOMENTS THEY'LL ALL EXPLODE -- SHATTERING THIS WORLD! SO-- SAVE YOURSELF, *GREEN LANTERN,* IF YOU CAN!

SAVE MYSELF? I'LL DO BETTER THAN THAT...

WITH A GIANT'S STRENGTH, THE MIGHTY POWER BEAM ONCE AGAIN IS BROUGHT INTO PLAY...

MY RING WILL TAKE US *ALL* BACK TO THE NORMAL WORLD--AND NORMAL SIZE AGAIN! JUST BRACE YOUR-SELVES--I'VE GOT TO ACT *FAST* BEFORE THE ROBOT-EXPLOSIONS CAN TAKE PLACE!

AND SPLIT-SECONDS LATER...

Whew!! THERE IT IS--THE ROBOTS HAVE EXPLODED!! AND EVEN THOUGH WE'VE ALREADY PASSED OUT OF THE *ATOM WORLD,* THE FORCE OF THE EXPLOSION IS SO GREAT THAT WE CAN HEAR IT-- AND FEEL IT--JUST BARELY!

14.

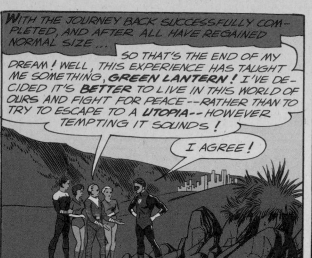

WITH THE JOURNEY BACK SUCCESSFULLY COMPLETED, AND AFTER ALL HAVE REGAINED NORMAL SIZE...

SO THAT'S THE END OF MY DREAM! WELL, THIS EXPERIENCE HAS TAUGHT ME SOMETHING, **GREEN LANTERN**! I'VE DECIDED IT'S **BETTER** TO LIVE IN THIS WORLD OF OURS AND FIGHT FOR PEACE--RATHER THAN TO TRY TO ESCAPE TO A **UTOPIA**--HOWEVER TEMPTING IT SOUNDS!

I AGREE!

I'M GLAD TO BE BACK TOO! THERE'S NOT ENOUGH TO DO IN A UTOPIA! I'M LOOKING FORWARD TO GETTING TO **WORK** AGAIN!

YOU'RE LOOKING FORWARD TO **SOMETHING ELSE** TOO, AREN'T YOU, WILL?

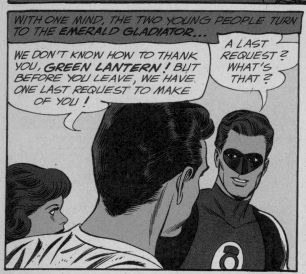

WITH ONE MIND, THE TWO YOUNG PEOPLE TURN TO THE **EMERALD GLADIATOR**...

WE DON'T KNOW HOW TO THANK YOU, **GREEN LANTERN**! BUT BEFORE YOU LEAVE, WE HAVE ONE LAST REQUEST TO MAKE OF YOU!

A LAST REQUEST? WHAT'S THAT?

AS THE JETPLANE CARRYING ACE TEST PILOT HAL JORDAN FLIES BACK TOWARD **FERRIS FIELD** LATER THAT DAY...

I'LL HAVE TO INVENT AN EXCUSE TO EXPLAIN WHY I HAVEN'T CONTACTED THE FIELD ALL MORNING! BUT ALSO I MUSTN'T FORGET ONE OTHER THING--THAT **GREEN LANTERN** HAS A DATE TO BE **BEST MAN** AT THE WEDDING OF WILL CHAMBERS AND BEVERLY BLANDING--ONE WEEK FROM TODAY!

The End

GREEN LANTERN

"IN BRIGHTEST DAY..."

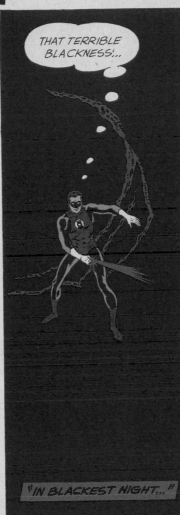

"IN BLACKEST NIGHT..."

"NO EVIL SHALL ESCAPE MY SIGHT!"

"IN BRIGHTEST DAY, IN BLACKEST NIGHT..." FAMILIAR WORDS--FROM GREEN LANTERN'S FAMOUS OATH TAKEN WHENEVER HE CHARGES HIS POWER RING! BUT DO THE LINES OF THAT SACRED VOW HAVE ANY SPECIAL MEANING? OR ARE THEY MERELY FINE-SOUNDING, EMPTY SYMBOLS? FOR THE STARTLING TRUTH WHICH IS GUARANTEED TO KEEP YOU ON TENTERHOOKS, READ...

The ORIGIN of GREEN LANTERN'S OATH!

IN THE DRESSING ROOM OF HAL [GREEN LANTERN] JORDAN, AT THE FERRIS AIRCRAFT COMPANY HANGAR, A MYSTIC CEREMONY TAKES PLACE WHICH NEVER FAILS TO FASCINATE PIEFACE, HAL'S ESKIMO MECHANIC, AND GL'S SOLE CONFIDANT...

IN BRIGHTEST DAY, IN BLACKEST NIGHT, NO EVIL SHALL ESCAPE MY SIGHT! LET THOSE WHO WORSHIP EVIL'S MIGHT BEWARE MY POWER -- GREEN LANTERN'S LIGHT!

AS THE EMERALD GLADIATOR TURNS, HIS RING CHARGED FOR ANOTHER TWENTY-FOUR HOURS...

GREEN LANTERN, YOU ALWAYS TAKE THAT OATH WHEN YOU CHARGE YOUR POWER RING! BUT WHERE DID THE OATH COME FROM? I'VE BEEN WONDERING ABOUT THAT!

SO IT'S AROUSED YOUR CURIOSITY, HAS IT, PIEFACE?

WELL, AS A MATTER OF FACT THERE'S A STORY BEHIND THAT OATH -- AND IF YOU WANT TO HEAR IT...

JUMPING FISH-HOOKS! YOU BET I DO!

I DIDN'T ALWAYS TAKE THE OATH! IN THE BEGINNING -- WHEN I FIRST RECEIVED MY RING AND POWER BATTERY FROM THE SPACEMAN WHO CRASHED ON EARTH* -- I SIMPLY CHARGED MY RING WITHOUT ANY OATH AT ALL! BUT THEN IN THAT FIRST WEEK I HAD THREE ADVENTURES...

*Editor's Note:

FULL DETAILS OF THIS EVENT WERE REVEALED IN THE GREEN LANTERN ORIGIN STORY, "SOS -- GREEN LANTERN!"

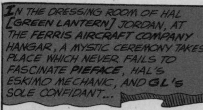 "THE FIRST OCCURRED HERE IN COAST CITY IN A BANK WHERE, AS HAL JORDAN, I HAD GONE TO MAKE A DEPOSIT..."

HELLO, MR. JORDAN! NICE TO SEE YOU AGAIN!

IT STILL GIVES ME A THRILL TO REALIZE THAT MR. BURBANK HASN'T THE LEAST IDEA OF MY SECRET IDENTITY...

BURBANK

NO ONE IN THE WORLD SUSPECTS THAT AT A MOMENT'S NOTICE I CAN BECOME MIGHTY GREEN LANTERN -- WITH MY AMAZING POWER RING AND INVINCIBLE GREEN BEAM! GOLLY, WHAT A FEELING IT IS!

"BUT WHAT I DIDN'T REALIZE AT THE TIME, IN THE STREET OUTSIDE..."

THIS IS A **BRIGHT DAY**, HANK! YOU SURE OUR SCHEME WILL WORK ON A DAY LIKE THIS?

DON'T WORRY...

WHEN THIS **SUPER-MAGNESIUM** BOMB GOES OFF AROUND HERE IT WILL MAKE THE SUN'S LIGHT LOOK LIKE CANDLEPOWER! WE'VE TESTED IT A DOZEN TIMES! IT CAN'T FAIL!

LET'S GO! CUT THE JAWING!

"THE NEXT MOMENT THE BOMB WAS THROWN FROM THE CAR, AND BEFORE ANYONE AROUND HAD TIME EVEN TO GET A GOOD LOOK AT IT..."

THAT INCREDIBLE LIGHT--!

BLINDING AH--!

HELP! WHERE AM I?

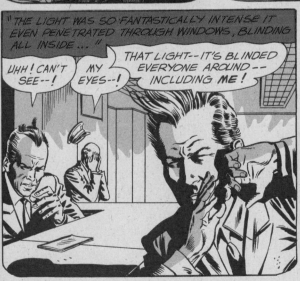

"THE LIGHT WAS SO FANTASTICALLY INTENSE IT EVEN PENETRATED THROUGH WINDOWS, BLINDING ALL INSIDE..."

UHH! CAN'T SEE--!

MY EYES--!

THAT LIGHT--IT'S BLINDED EVERYONE AROUND-- INCLUDING ME!

"WITH PLANNED PRECISION, THE CROOKS PILED OUT OF THEIR CAR, WEARING **SPECIAL GOGGLES** TO PROTECT THEM FROM THE AWFUL GLARE..."

INTO THE BANK, BOYS!

IT'S WORKING LIKE A CHARM! THIS IS GOING TO BE LIKE TAKING PENNIES FROM A **BLIND MAN**!

COAST CITY BANK

3

"IN NO TIME THE BANK HAD BEEN LOOTED! UNABLE TO SEE, I STILL HEARD THINGS SO I COULD PIECE TOGETHER WHAT WAS HAPPENING..."

WE'VE GOT THE LOOT! NOW BACK TO THE CAR-- HUSTLE!

A ROBBERY!? THE CROOKS MUST HAVE CAUSED THAT TERRIBLE LIGHT SOMEHOW-- TO AID THEM IN THEIR CRIME! I'VE GOT TO STOP THEM!

"INSTINCTIVELY I ACTED, FAST AS I COULD..."

IT'S SAFE TO CHANGE TO MY GREEN LANTERN COSTUME RIGHT HERE--BECAUSE EVERYONE AROUND IS BLINDED JUST LIKE I AM! BUT EVEN AS GL, I STILL CAN'T SEE--SO HOW CAN I CORRAL THOSE THIEVES?

"OUT IN THE STREET THE ANSWER CAME TO ME IN ONE OF THOSE FLASHES OF INSIGHT YOU GET IN ACTION! I USED MY POWER RING LIKE A RADAR TRANSMITTER..."

MY FANTASTIC GREEN BEAM IS THROWING OUT WAVES JUST LIKE A RADAR SET--AND IMAGES OF EVERYTHING AROUND ME ARE COMING BACK TO ME AND ENTERING MY BRAIN--SO I CAN ACTUALLY "SEE" THOSE THREE CROOKS DASHING FOR THEIR CAR NOW!

"ONCE I WORKED OUT THE 'RADAR-METHOD,' CAPTURING THE CROOKS WAS EASY, EVEN WITHOUT THE USE OF MY EYES!"

THE UNBREAKABLE NET FORMED BY MY GREEN BEAM HAS MADE ONE OF THE CROOKS HELPLESS! NOW FOR THE OTHER TWO!

ULP--HOW DID I GET IN THIS MESS?

UGH! SOMETHING HAS WHIRLED US AROUND-- WRAPPED AGAINST THIS LAMPPOST--

--AND HANDCUFFED US TOGETHER HERE! WE--WE CAN'T MOVE!

4

Panel 1 (caption): "AFTER THAT IT WAS EASY TO HOLD THE THIEVES HELPLESS UNTIL POLICE WERE SUMMONED TO ARREST THEM..."

Panel 1 (speech): YES, EVENTUALLY WE ALL RECOVERED OUR SIGHT, PIEFACE! BUT THAT INCIDENT STILL DIDN'T GIVE ME MY OATH! THE OATH ITSELF DIDN'T OCCUR TO ME UNTIL AFTER THE **THIRD** ADVENTURE! BUT BEFORE I GET TO THAT I MUST TELL YOU ABOUT THE **SECOND** ONE...

Panel 2 (caption): "IT WAS A DAY OR SO LATER AND I HAD JUST DELIVERED AN EXPERIMENTAL PLANE--AS HAL JORDAN, OF COURSE--BACK TO THE FACTORY."

Panel 2 (speech): WE'RE GOING TO KNOCK DOWN THIS ENGINE AND REBUILD IT FROM SCRATCH FOR YOU, MR. JORDAN! IT WON'T TAKE LONG!

GOOD! I'LL CHECK IN WITH YOU TOMORROW, MR. DAVIS!

Panel 3 (caption): "THE WAIT GAVE ME SOME TIME TO MYSELF IN SAN SIERRO WHERE THE FACTORY WAS. THAT NIGHT, AT MY HOTEL, THE DESK CLERK AND I BECAME FRIENDLY..."

Panel 3 (speech): TRAIN ROBBERIES-- IN THIS DAY AND AGE!?

THEY'RE A DARING BAND, MR. JORDAN...

Newspaper: LATE NEWS — TRAIN ROBBERS STRIKE AGAIN!

Panel 4 (speech): AND THE ODD THING IS THE POLICE KNOW WHERE THEIR HIDEOUT IS-- OUT IN SIERRO HILLS! BUT IT DOESN'T HELP THEM! EVERY TIME THE GANG REACHES THE HIDEOUT, NOBODY CAN FOLLOW THEM!

WOULD YOU MIND EXPLAINING THAT?

Panel 5 (caption): "AND SOON AFTER, A FIGURE NEVER BEFORE SEEN AROUND SAN SIERRO WAS HEADING FOR THE HILLS AT JET-SPEED."

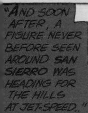

Panel 5 (speech): ACCORDING TO THAT DESK CLERK, THE TRAIN-ROBBING BAND IS A THROWBACK TO THE OLD DAYS-- OPERATING ON HORSEBACK LIKE GANGS OF THE OLD WEST! AND THEIR HIDEOUT IS AN UNDERGROUND NETWORK OF CAVES HERE IN SIERRO HILLS...

Panel 6 (thought): I SHOULD BE NEAR THEIR HIDEOUT--EH? THERE'S THE GANG NOW! THEY MUST BE RETURNING FROM A FORAY--AND THEY'RE ABOUT TO ENTER THAT CAVE OPENING!

5

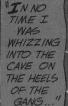

"IN NO TIME I WAS WHIZZING INTO THE CAVE ON THE HEELS OF THE GANG..."

THE CLERK DESCRIBED THE **BLACKNESS** IN THIS CAVE AS **UN-BELIEVABLY DENSE**-- AND NOW I KNOW WHAT HE MEANS! THE ROBBERS HAVE MEMO-RIZED EVERY FOOT OF THIS PLACE SO THEY CAN MOVE THROUGH IT...

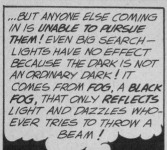

...BUT ANYONE ELSE COMING IN IS **UNABLE TO PURSUE THEM**! EVEN BIG SEARCH-LIGHTS HAVE NO EFFECT BECAUSE THE DARK IS NOT AN ORDINARY DARK! IT COMES FROM **FOG**, A **BLACK FOG**, THAT ONLY **REFLECTS** LIGHT AND DAZZLES WHO-EVER TRIES TO THROW A BEAM!

"BEING A NOVICE WITH THE **POWER RING**, I WAS AT THAT TIME **UNABLE** TO OVER-COME THE OBSTACLE.."

I CAN'T SUMMON UP ENOUGH POWER TO THROW A LIGHT THAT WILL PENETRATE THIS TERRIBLE FOG! BUT I--I CAN'T ADMIT DEFEAT! I'VE GOT TO BRING THOSE TRICKY LAW-BREAKERS TO JUSTICE!

"SUDDENLY A WAY OUT OF MY DILEMMA OCCURRED TO ME..."

THOSE CROOKS ARE IN HERE SOMEWHERE! BUT INSTEAD OF TRYING TO SEE THEM IN THIS INCREDIBLE DARK, WHAT I'VE GOT TO DO IS MAKE **THEM** SUPER-VISIBLE!

"BACKING MY RING WITH ALL MY WILL POWER, I SHOT OUT WAVES OF THE GREEN BEAM ALL AROUND ME, AND WHERE IT STRUCK THE CROOKS IT MADE EACH OF THEM **PHOSPHORESCENT**..."

HEY, I'M GLOWING--

IT'S WORK-ING! BY MAKING THE THIEVES **GLOW** WITH PHOSPHORESCENCE I'VE MADE THEM SO BRIGHT THAT I CAN SEE THEM EVEN THROUGH THE FOG!! NOW TO GO INTO ACTION--!

6

"AS I CAME AT THEM, THE FRENZIED CROOKS FIRED AROUND THEM BLINDLY, BUT MY RING PROTECTED ME..."

I CAN CREATE SUCH **HEAT** WITH MY RING THAT IT **MELTS DOWN** THE BULLETS COMING AT ME IN MIDAIR!

AND THAT, **PIEFACE**, WAS THE **FIRST TIME** I'D EVER USED MY RING TO STOP BULLETS! AND NATURALLY THE SENSATION WAS A BIG THRILL FOR ME!

GOLLY! I CAN SEE HOW IT WOULD BE!

"AS SOON AS MY FOES HAD RUN OUT OF AMMUNITION, I SETTLED MATTERS SWIFTLY..."

THESE BANDITS MAY ROB TRAINS LIKE THE OLD WEST--BUT THEY'RE GOING TO JAIL IN ULTRA-MODERN STYLE-- ON **GREEN LANTERN'S** POWER BEAM!

THAT WAS THE **SECOND** ADVENTURE, **PIEFACE!** BUT YOU WON'T UNDERSTAND COMPLETELY ABOUT MY OATH UNTIL I'VE RELATED THE **THIRD** ONE TO YOU! THAT TOOK PLACE BEFORE YOU CAME TO WORK HERE AT THE **FERRIS AIRCRAFT COMPANY...**

"ONE DAY, AS HAL JORDAN, I WALKED INTO THE OFFICE TO FIND..."

WHAT'S THAT, CAROL? YOU SAY THE **OFFICE SAFE** HAS BEEN STOLEN?

THAT'S RIGHT, HAL! IT CONTAINED A LARGE SUM IN CASH, THE COMPANY PAYROLL!

25

"EXCITING AS CAROL'S NEWS WAS, I STILL COULDN'T HELP NOTICING HOW PRETTY SHE WAS!"

APPARENTLY THE THIEVES COULDN'T OPEN THE SAFE HERE, SO AFTER WORKING PART OF THE NIGHT THEY MANAGED TO GET THE SAFE INTO A TRUCK AND DROVE OFF WITH IT! THE POLICE HAVEN'T BEEN ABLE TO TRACE THEM YET!

"I FOUND SOME EXCUSE TO SLIP AWAY. AND SOON AFTER, RIGHT HERE IN MY DRESSING ROOM, I CHANGED..."

"THEN, AS GREEN LANTERN, I SET OFF TO FIND THAT SAFE AND THE CROOKS WHO HAD MADE OFF WITH IT..."

NO SIGN OF THEM! AND YET THEY WOULDN'T HAVE GONE VERY FAR! THEY'D JUST GET OUT INTO THE COUNTRY SOMEWHERE WHERE THEY COULD BLOW THE SAFE OPEN WITHOUT ATTRACTING ATTENTION! WAIT--

"MY OWN THOUGHTS GAVE ME A CLUE..."

JUST SEARCHING AIMLESSLY THIS WAY MAY NOT BE BEST! THE CROOKS COULD GET THE SAFE OPEN AND TAKE OFF WITH THE PAYROLL LONG BEFORE I FIND THEM! I'VE GOT ANOTHER IDEA!

"...AND CHARGED MY RING! YOU SEE, AT THAT TIME I STILL TOOK NO OATH, BUT STILL I MADE A KIND OF SILENT VOW AGAINST EVIL-DOERS..."

"WHAT I DID WAS TO USE MY POWER BEAM TO THROW A WIDE BELT OF RADIATION ALL AROUND THE FERRIS COMPANY AREA..."

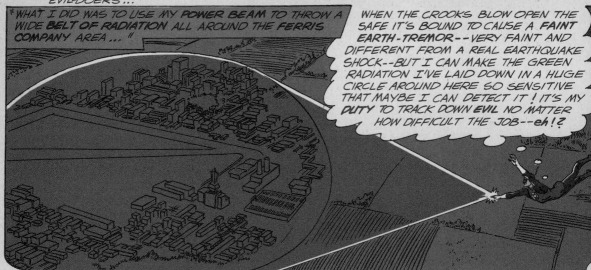

WHEN THE CROOKS BLOW OPEN THE SAFE IT'S BOUND TO CAUSE A FAINT EARTH-TREMOR--VERY FAINT AND DIFFERENT FROM A REAL EARTHQUAKE SHOCK--BUT I CAN MAKE THE GREEN RADIATION I'VE LAID DOWN IN A HUGE CIRCLE AROUND HERE SO SENSITIVE THAT MAYBE I CAN DETECT IT! IT'S MY DUTY TO TRACK DOWN EVIL NO MATTER HOW DIFFICULT THE JOB--EH!?

"JUST AS I LAID DOWN MY CIRCLE OF RADIATION, THE THING HAPPENED..."

THERE IT IS! MY BEAM IS PICKING UP AN EARTH-TREMOR--COMING FROM THE SOUTHWEST!

"I SHOT OFF IN THE DIRECTION OF THE TREMOR WITH AS MUCH SPEED AS MY POWER RING COULD MUSTER..."

THE LITTLE SHOCK IS COMING FROM THE DUNE COUNTRY--A SORT OF DESERT WHERE NO ONE LIVES! AND THAT FITS IN--IT'S THE KIND OF PLACE WHERE THE CROOKS WOULD GO TO BLOW THE SAFE!

"AND MOMENTS LATER I BURST UPON THEM..."

GOT HERE JUST IN TIME! THEY'VE DYNAMITED THE SAFE ALL RIGHT, BUT THEY HAVEN'T GOT THE PAYROLL OUT YET--AND IF I HAVE ANYTHING TO SAY ABOUT IT THEY NEVER WILL!

SOMETHING'S COMIN' AT US, HANK!

"THE FIGHT WAS FAST, FURIOUS--AND SHORT..."

THOSE EXPLOSIVE SHOTS CREATED BY MY GREEN BEAM WON'T HURT THE CROOKS--BUT THEY WILL KNOCK THEM COLD--

--AND ENABLE ME TO TRANSPORT THEM--AND THEIR LOOT--THE WHOLE KIT AND KABOODLE--BACK TO TOWN WITHOUT ANY TROUBLE!

9

SO THERE YOU HAVE THE *THREE ADVENTURES* WHICH INSPIRED MY OATH, *PIEFACE!* BUT MAYBE I'D BETTER EXPLAIN...

NO, WAIT! LET ME TRY, *GREEN LANTERN!* I THINK I CAN UNDERSTAND...

As THE GOOD-HUMORED FACE OF THE ESKIMO GREASEMONKEY GLEAMS WITH SUDDEN COMPREHENSION...

"IN BRIGHTEST DAY..."--THAT REFERS TO THE *FIRST ADVENTURE* WHERE THE MAGNESIUM BOMB MADE A LIGHT SO BRIGHT IT BLINDED EVERYONE AROUND!

GOOD! THAT'S RIGHT, *PIE!*

AND *"IN BLACKEST NIGHT..."*--THAT REFERS TO THE INCIDENT IN THE CAVE IN *SIERRO HILLS* WHERE THE FOGGY DARKNESS WAS SO BLACK THAT NOT EVEN LIGHT OR YOUR RING COULD PENETRATE IT!

EXACTLY!

AND *"NO EVIL SHALL ESCAPE MY SIGHT"*--THAT OBVIOUSLY COMES FROM THE LAST ADVENTURE WHERE AGAINST ODDS YOU DETECTED THOSE CROOKS WHO THOUGHT THEY HAD ESCAPED JUSTICE AND THE LAW!

CORRECT! THEN ALL I DID WAS ADD THE *LAST TWO LINES* TO MAKE IT RHYME! AND SO NOW YOU KNOW THE WHOLE STORY OF MY OATH, *PIEFACE!*

IN BRIGHTEST DAY, IN BLACKEST NIGHT, NO EVIL SHALL ESCAPE MY SIGHT! LET THOSE WHO WORSHIP EVIL'S MIGHT BEWARE MY POWER-- *GREEN LANTERN'S LIGHT!*

The End

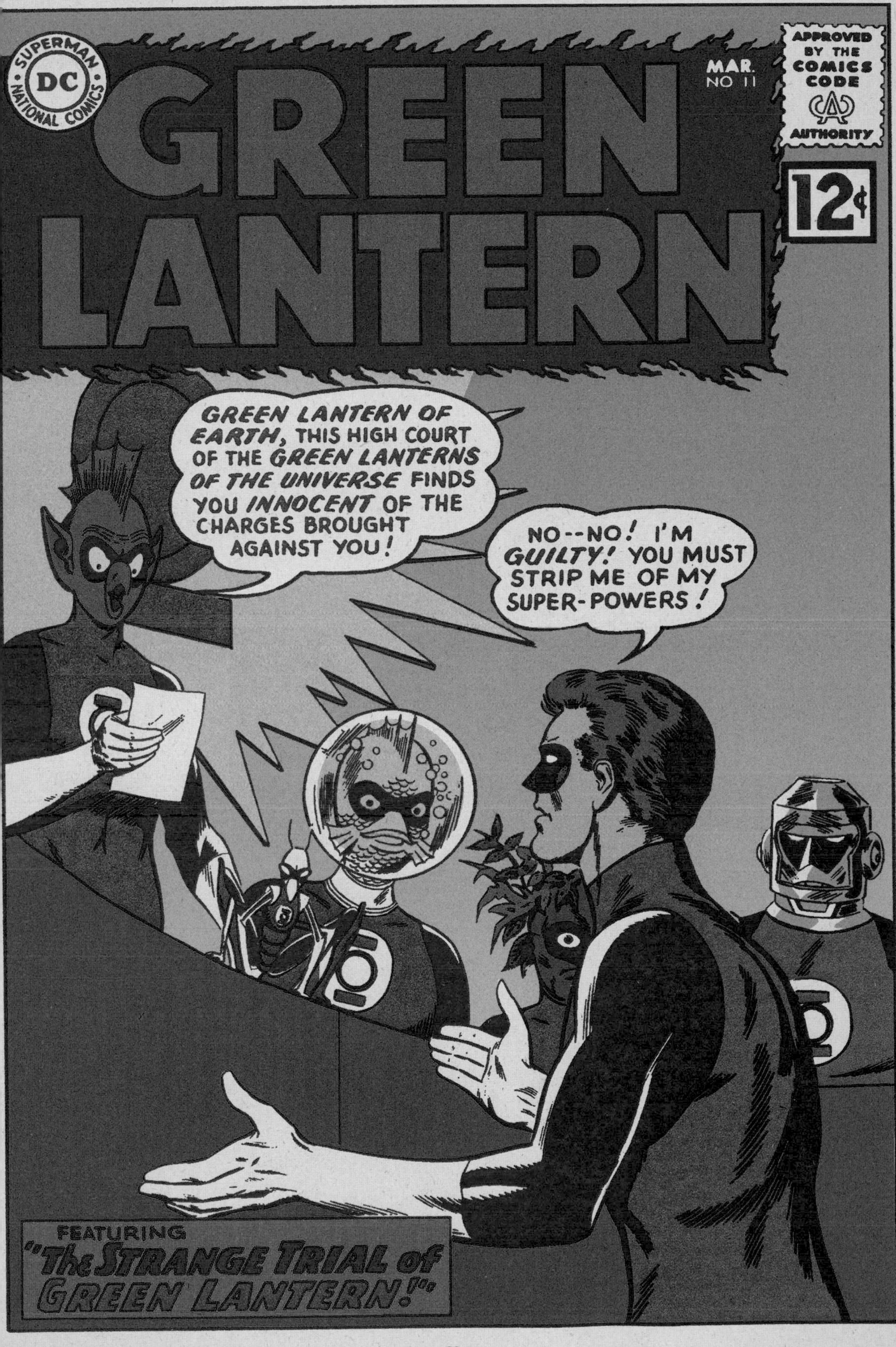
SUPERMAN DC NATIONAL COMICS
GREEN LANTERN
MAR. NO 11
APPROVED BY THE COMICS CODE AUTHORITY
12¢
GREEN LANTERN OF EARTH, THIS HIGH COURT OF THE GREEN LANTERNS OF THE UNIVERSE FINDS YOU INNOCENT OF THE CHARGES BROUGHT AGAINST YOU!
NO--NO! I'M GUILTY! YOU MUST STRIP ME OF MY SUPER-POWERS!
FEATURING "The STRANGE TRIAL of GREEN LANTERN!"

GREEN LANTERN

INCREDIBLE AS IT MAY SEEM, THE ABOVE SCENE IS A TRUE ONE! YET HOW EXPLAIN IT? AND HOW EXPLAIN, FURTHER, THE OTHER PUZZLING ACTS OF THE EMERALD GLADIATOR THAT VERY WEEK, ALL OF THE SAME CALIBER, WHEN HE VIOLATED HIS OWN HIGH CODE OF BEHAVIOR TIME AND AGAIN? WHATEVER THE REASON BEHIND GREEN LANTERN'S STARTLING ACTIONS, THEY LED INEVITABLY TO THE HIGH COURT OF ALL THE GREEN LANTERNS OF THE COSMOS, WHERE TOOK PLACE IN DUE COURSE...

The STRANGE TRIAL OF GREEN LANTERN!

GREEN LANTERN, THAT WINDOW-CLEANER'S BELT JUST SNAPPED! HE'S FALLING TO HIS DEATH! GO INTO ACTION!

HURRY! THERE'S STILL TIME! USE YOUR POWER RING TO SAVE HIM, GREEN LANTERN! JUST DON'T STAND THERE!

IN THE FAR-OFF PLANET OF *YQUEM* SOMEWHERE IN THE MILKY WAY GALAXY AN EXTRAORDINARY TRIAL IS TAKING PLACE! A PICKED ASSEMBLAGE OF *GREEN LANTERNS*, FROM VARIOUS SECTORS OF THE COSMOS, IS SITTING IN SOLEMN JUDGMENT ON ONE OF ITS OWN MEMBERS...

WE ARE READY TO HAND DOWN OUR DECISION ON YOU, *GREEN LANTERN* OF *EARTH!* BUT BEFORE WE DO, LET US REVIEW YOUR AMAZING CASE! FIRST OF ALL, IN VIEW OF YOUR SPOTLESS RECORD UP TO NOW, IT WAS DECIDED BY THE *GUARDIANS** THAT YOU WOULD BE TRIED BY US -- A JURY OF YOUR PEERS AND EQUALS!

* *Editor's Note:* THE *MYSTERIOUS GUARDIANS OF THE UNIVERSE* FROM WHOM ALL THE *GREEN LANTERNS* DERIVE THEIR *POWER BATTERIES* AND ALL THE OTHER ASPECTS OF THEIR *SUPER-POWERS!*

AND NOW TO SUM UP THE CHARGES AGAINST YOU! IT IS ALLEGED -- AND YOU HAVE *ADMITTED* -- THAT YOU FAILED TO USE YOUR *POWER RING* AND *BEAM* IN THE BEST TRADITION OF OUR ORGANIZATION! THERE WERE THREE SPECIFIC INSTANCES OF THIS MISCONDUCT -- ALL CONFIRMED BY YOU!

"IN THE FIRST INSTANCE, BACK ON YOUR HOME PLANET OF *EARTH*, YOU USED YOUR *POWER RING* TO BREAK INTO A BANK, EVEN THOUGH THERE WAS *NO CRIME* GOING ON THERE AT THE TIME..."

GREEN LANTERN? MUST BE BANK ROBBERS AROUND--

"RUTHLESSLY YOU TRANS-FIXED ALL THE TELLERS AND DEPOSITORS PRESENT, TEMPORARILY PARALYZING THEM WITH A SWEEP OF YOUR GREEN BEAM..."

HE MUST BE THE BANK ROBBER!

GREAT SCOTT! HE'S HEADING FOR THE VAULT!

"THERE WAS MUCH MONEY IN THE VAULT! YOU OPENED IT! BUT THEN AT THE LAST MOMENT YOU SEEMED TO CHANGE YOUR MIND..."

FIRST SECURITY BANK

"YOU SUDDENLY PLUNGED OFF AND ON YOUR WAY, EMPTY-HANDED! THAT MUCH HAS BEEN ESTABLISHED!"

2

THE SECOND INSTANCE OCCURRED SHORTLY AFTER THE FIRST ONE! AT A GALA ENTERTAINMENT FOR CHARITY IN **COAST CITY** IT WAS AGREED THAT EVERYONE WHO ATTENDED, WITHOUT EXCEPTION, SHOULD PAY THE $100 ENTRANCE FEE INTO THE HALL! BUT WHEN **YOU** ARRIVED...

".YOU HAD NO TICKET! THE MAN AT THE DOOR TRIED TO STOP YOU.."

HOLD ON, **GREEN LANTERN!** YOU MUST PAY TO GET IN -- JUST LIKE ANYONE ELSE!

YOU DARE TO **STOP ME?**

"IT WAS A BALEFUL GLANCE YOU DIRECTED AT THE TICKET-TAKER..."

DO YOU REALIZE I COULD USE MY **POWER RING** TO TURN THIS WHOLE HALL **UPSIDE-DOWN** IF I WANTED TO?

I--I'M SURE YOU COULD! B-BUT YOU'VE **STILL** GOT TO PAY YOUR WAY IN!

"THE NEXT MOMENT..."

I'LL TEACH YOU TO--

HELP!!

"SUDDENLY, ONCE AGAIN, YOU SEEMED TO REGAIN CONTROL OF YOURSELF! AND..."

GREAT THUNDER! WHAT IN THE WORLD HAS COME OVER **GREEN LANTERN!?** I NEVER SAW HIM ACT THAT WAY BEFORE! BUT AT LEAST-- HE DIDN'T HURT ME!

"BUT THE THIRD CASE CITED AGAINST YOU IS THE MOST **SERIOUS** OF ALL! IT WAS LATER IN THE SAME DAY AND YOU WERE PASSING A BUSY THOROUGHFARE..."

LOOK! OH-- SAVE HIM, SOME- BODY!

3

A WINDOW-CLEANER'S BELT HAD BROKEN! HE WAS CLINGING TO A LEDGE IN DIRE PERIL...

HE'S WEAKENING! HE'S LOSING HIS GRIP--!

"BUT THEN, SOME ON THE STREET SAW YOU BEHIND THEM..."

IT--IT'S GREEN LANTERN!

HURRY, GREEN LANTERN! SAVE THAT MAN!

"BUT INCREDIBLY, YOU JUST STOOD THERE! YOU DIDN'T MAKE A MOVE..."

GREEN LANTERN, DON'T YOU UNDERSTAND? THAT MAN UP THERE-- HE'S ABOUT TO FALL --

HE IS FALLING!!

"EVEN THEN, EVEN AT THAT CRITICAL INSTANT, YOU STILL MADE NO MOVE TO SAVE THE UNFORTUNATE WORKER..."

AHHH!

GREEN LANTERN-- DO SOMETHING!

"ONLY AT THE VERY LAST INSTANT DID YOUR MAGIC BEAM FINALLY SHOOT OUT TO FORM A BED OF SPRINGS UNDER THE PLUNGING MAN AND CUSHION HIS FALL SO THAT HE LANDED UNHURT!"

WHEW!! I THOUGHT SURE HE WAS A GONER!

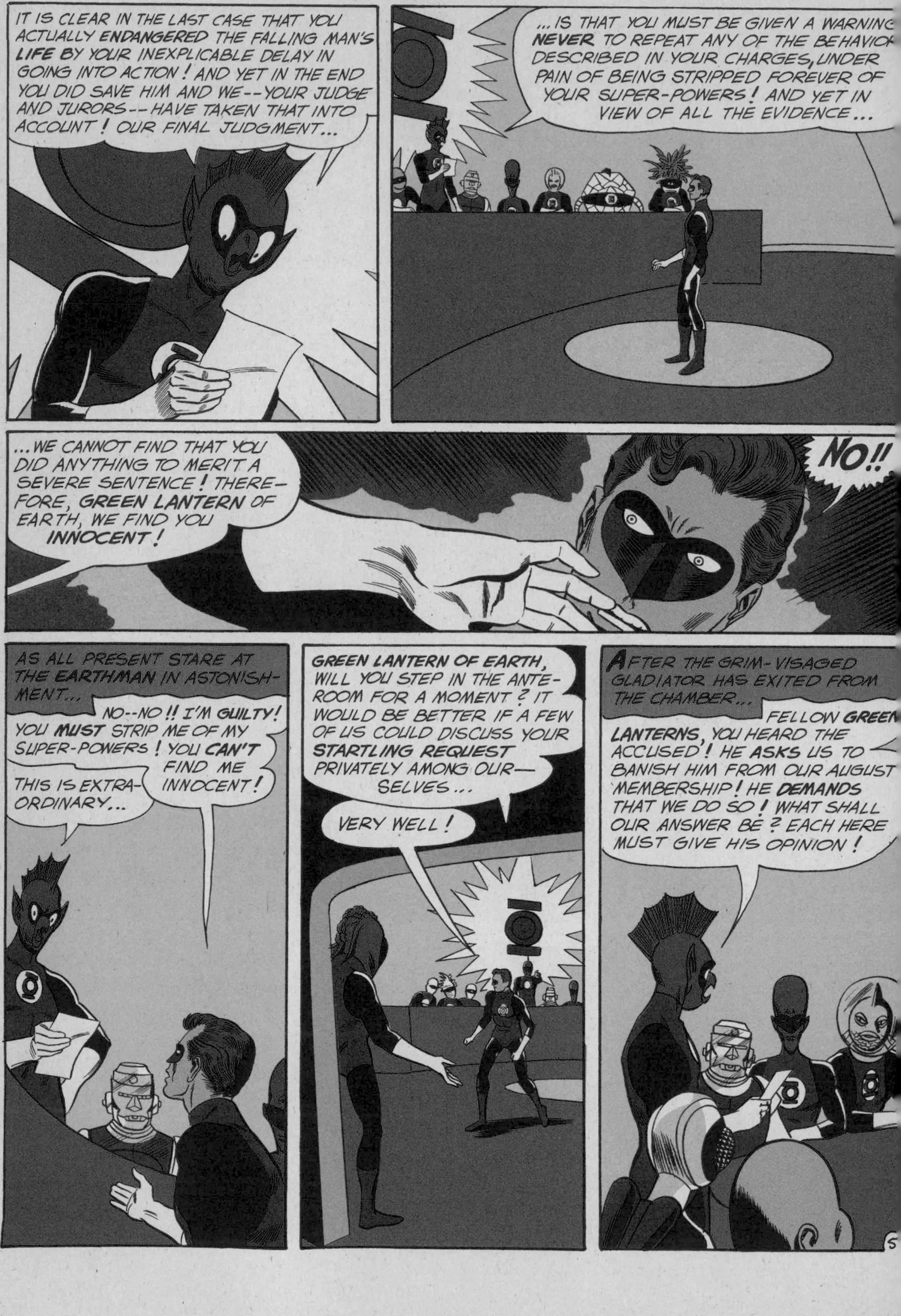
IT IS CLEAR IN THE LAST CASE THAT YOU ACTUALLY ENDANGERED THE FALLING MAN'S LIFE BY YOUR INEXPLICABLE DELAY IN GOING INTO ACTION! AND YET IN THE END YOU DID SAVE HIM AND WE--YOUR JUDGE AND JURORS--HAVE TAKEN THAT INTO ACCOUNT! OUR FINAL JUDGMENT...
...IS THAT YOU MUST BE GIVEN A WARNING NEVER TO REPEAT ANY OF THE BEHAVIOR DESCRIBED IN YOUR CHARGES, UNDER PAIN OF BEING STRIPPED FOREVER OF YOUR SUPER-POWERS! AND YET IN VIEW OF ALL THE EVIDENCE...
...WE CANNOT FIND THAT YOU DID ANYTHING TO MERIT A SEVERE SENTENCE! THEREFORE, GREEN LANTERN OF EARTH, WE FIND YOU INNOCENT!
NO!!
AS ALL PRESENT STARE AT THE EARTHMAN IN ASTONISHMENT...
NO--NO!! I'M GUILTY! YOU MUST STRIP ME OF MY SUPER-POWERS! YOU CAN'T FIND ME INNOCENT!
THIS IS EXTRAORDINARY...
GREEN LANTERN OF EARTH, WILL YOU STEP IN THE ANTEROOM FOR A MOMENT? IT WOULD BE BETTER IF A FEW OF US COULD DISCUSS YOUR STARTLING REQUEST PRIVATELY AMONG OURSELVES...
VERY WELL!
AFTER THE GRIM-VISAGED GLADIATOR HAS EXITED FROM THE CHAMBER...
FELLOW GREEN LANTERNS, YOU HEARD THE ACCUSED! HE ASKS US TO BANISH HIM FROM OUR AUGUST MEMBERSHIP! HE DEMANDS THAT WE DO SO! WHAT SHALL OUR ANSWER BE? EACH HERE MUST GIVE HIS OPINION!
5

SLOWLY, WEIGHING THEIR WORDS, THE MEMBERS OF THE INTERGALACTIC BAND ONE BY ONE RENDER THEIR VERDICT! AMONG THEM...

GREEN LANTERN OF GRENDA, A WORLD WHERE ROBOTS REIGN!

I SAY THERE MUST BE A GOOD REASON FOR THE INCREDIBLE REQUEST OF GREEN LANTERN OF EARTH! WE SHOULD NOT GO AGAINST HIS WISHES!

GREEN LANTERN OF AEROS, A WATER WORLD INHABITED BY VARIOUS FORMS OF FISH LIFE!

I AGREE!

GREEN LANTERN OF ROJIRA, ONE OF THE MOST FUTURISTIC, SUPER-SCIENTIFIC AND AGED CIVILIZATIONS IN EXISTENCE!

THERE MAY BE MORE HERE THAN MEETS THE EYE!

GREEN LANTERN OF JS86, WHERE INTELLI-GENT PLANT LIFE HAS ARRIVED AT A STAGE FAR ADVANCED OVER THAT KNOWN ANY — WHERE ELSE!

LET US DO AS HE SAYS--TERRIBLE AS HIS FATE WILL BE!

GREEN LANTERN OF BARRIO III, A WORLD IN WHICH CRYSTAL LIFE FORMS HAVE ATTAINED DOMINANCE. AN ULTRASENSITIVE FORM WITH 13 SENSES INSTEAD OF THE USUAL 6 OF HUMANS!

AGREED!

TOMAR RE, GREEN LANTERN OF XUDAR, WHERE BIRD-LIFE HAS BECOME THE MASTER SPECIES!

I SEE THAT BEHIND OUR WORDS WE ALL HAVE THE SAME IDEA IN MIND, FELLOW GREEN LANTERNS! THEREFORE... OUR DECISION IS UNANIMOUS!

AND SOON, WITH HIS POWER RING TAKEN AWAY, THE INSIGNIA OF HIS FORMER RANK STRIPPED FROM HIM, ALONE, HAGGARD AND HELPLESS, THE ERSTWHILE EMERALD GLADIATOR IS CATAPULTED OFF YQUEM AND SENT ON A LONELY AND GRIM JOURNEY...

BY THE EARTHMAN'S OWN REQUEST, THE EX-GREEN LANTERN IS BEING TELE-PORTED BY OUR POWER BEAMS OUT OF THIS UNIVERSE ENTIRELY-- AND INTO THE EVIL ANTIMATTER UNIVERSE OF QWARD!

MAY HE NOT REGRET THAT REQUEST!

WE HAD NO CHOICE BUT TO GRANT IT!

6.

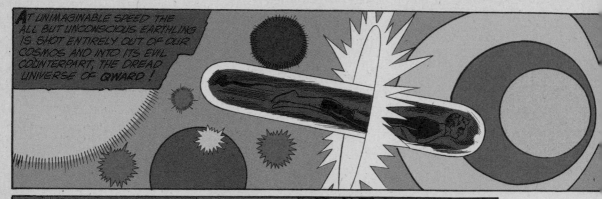

AT UNIMAGINABLE SPEED THE ALL BUT UNCONSCIOUS EARTHLING IS SHOT ENTIRELY OUT OF OUR COSMOS AND INTO ITS EVIL COUNTERPART, THE DREAD UNIVERSE OF QWARD!

AND AT THAT VERY MOMENT...

HERE COMES *GREEN LANTERN!* MY PLAN IS *SUCCEEDING* BETTER THAN I HAD DREAMED! AND NOW THAT HE IS IN *QWARD* MY *YELLOW BEAM* CAN TAKE *CONTROL* OF HIM-- AND GLIDE HIM HERE TO ME!!

*T*HUS IT IS THAT WHEN *GREEN LANTERN* HAS FINALLY COME TO REST, AND THE GREEN PROTECTIVE SHEATH AROUND HIM HAS DISSOLVED AWAY, HIS STARTLED EYES FALL ON NONE OTHER THAN HIS INCREDIBLE ARCH-ENEMY...

SINESTRO!? THE RENEGADE GREEN LANTERN OF THE PLANET KORUGAR!

GREETINGS, *GREEN LANTERN* OF EARTH! WELCOME TO *QWARD!* I DON'T WONDER THAT YOU'RE SURPRISED TO SEE ME--

--SINCE THE LAST TIME YOU SAW ME I WAS "ABSOLUTELY HELPLESS" IN THAT "IM-PENETRABLE" GREEN CAPSULE ORBITING YOUR UNIVERSE!* NO DOUBT YOU'RE EATEN UP WITH CURIOSITY TO LEARN HOW I MADE MY ESCAPE!

*Editor's Note! SEE STORY ENTITLED "THE BATTLE OF THE POWER RINGS" IN GREEN LANTERN #9!

BUT EVEN IF YOU AREN'T, MY FRIEND, I INTEND TO TELL YOU! SIT DOWN!

UHH! WITHOUT MY RING I'M POWERLESS AGAINST THAT *YELLOW BEAM* OF HIS!

7

NATURALLY WHEN YOU AND THE OTHER GREEN LANTERNS PUT ME IN THAT CAPSULE YOU TOOK AWAY *MY POWER RING!* YOU THOUGHT THAT WOULD PREVENT ME FROM EVER GETTING LOOSE! BUT THERE WAS ONE THING YOU OVERLOOKED...

"NO SOONER WAS I OUT OF YOUR SIGHT THAN I REACHED DOWN INTO A SECRET COMPARTMENT OF MY BOOT, AND THERE MY FINGERS CLOSED ON..."

MY *SPARE POWER RING!* HA! HA! HA! NATURALLY, BEING *SINESTRO*, I WAS WELL-HEELED WITH A SPARE-- FOR JUST SUCH A SITUATION AS THIS!

"AFTER THAT I SIMPLY CONVERTED THE CAPSULE INTO A *ROCKET* WITH MY YELLOW BEAM..."

"...AND PILOTED IT TOWARD *QWARD* AND HOME!"

SIMPLE, EH? AND SINCE YOU AND YOUR FELLOW *GREEN LANTERNS* CONSIDERED ME FINISHED, I HAD PLENTY OF TIME TO DREAM UP MY *REVENGE*--FIRST OF ALL AGAINST *YOU*, MY PARTICULAR FOE! TO BEGIN WITH...

...I USED MY EVIL *POWER RING* TO HELP ME BUILD THIS *MIND-CONTROL RAY-DEVICE!* IT HAS AN EFFECT SIMILAR TO HYPNOSIS, BUT WORKS AT ANY DISTANCE! AND BY MEANS OF IT I WAS ABLE...

...TO *GAIN* CONTROL OVER YOUR MIND, MY FRIEND!

UH--I'M BEGINNING TO SEE--!

8.

"IN ALL OF THESE CASES YOU WERE ACTING UNDER THE INFLUENCE OF MY RAY-DEVICE!"

I UNDERSTAND! BUT LIKE HYPNOSIS, YOUR RAY-DEVICE COULD NOT ACTUALLY FORCE ME TO DO ANYTHING WRONG-- SO THAT EACH TIME MY OWN SELF--MY BETTER SELF--WON OUT!

EXACTLY! AND YET--

IT WAS I WHO WON! FOR YOU DID ENOUGH TO BE BROUGHT UP ON CHARGES-- AS I HOPED YOU WOULD BE! AND THEN WHEN YOU WERE DECLARED INNOCENT BY THE HIGH COUNCIL OF GREEN LANTERNS-- WHO DO YOU THINK PLANTED IN YOUR MIND THE IMPULSE TO DECLARE YOURSELF GUILTY?

WHY... THAT LITTLE OLD EVIL-MAKER, SINESTRO!

I'VE STILL GOT THE USE OF MY HANDS... AND IF I CAN JUST REACH HIM...

DON'T TRY IT! MY YELLOW BEAM WOULD PULVERIZE YOU BEFORE YOU LEFT THAT CHAIR!

LISTEN! DON'T YOU REALIZE I COULD HAVE DESTROYED YOU AS SOON AS I GOT YOU HERE, GREEN LANTERN? BUT I HAD A REASON FOR TELLING YOU WHAT I DID--AND FOR FREEING YOUR BRAIN FROM MY MIND-CONTROL DEVICE! FOR ONE THING I WANTED YOU TO FULLY APPRECIATE MY CLEVERNESS...

BUT ALSO--I HAVE A MORE SINISTER IDEA! YOU AND I HAVE A GREAT DEAL IN COMMON NOW! WE BOTH ARE RENEGADE GREEN LANTERNS! WE HAVE BOTH BEEN BANISHED TO QWARD! DO YOU REALIZE--TOGETHER-- WITH YOUR ABILITIES ADDED TO MINE WHAT WE COULD ACCOMPLISH

?!

I AM OFFERING YOU A FULL PARTNERSHIP IN MY *CRUSADE OF EVIL*, GREEN LANTERN! TOGETHER WE CAN DESTROY THE *GUARDIANS OF THE UNIVERSE* AND ESTABLISH OURSELVES IN POWER IN THEIR PLACE! THERE IS NO LIMIT TO THE HEIGHTS WE CAN ATTAIN! BUT--

-- IF YOU *REFUSE*, THE PENALTY IS *DEATH*! MAKE YOUR CHOICE-- YOU HAVE EXACTLY FIVE SECONDS!

I DON'T NEED FIVE SECONDS!

IN THE FACE OF OVER-WHELMING ODDS, THE EX-GLADIATOR REVEALS THAT HE HAS NOT LOST A WHIT OF HIS BLAZING COURAGE...

COMING AT ME!? SO THAT'S YOUR ANSWER, eh? I CAN'T MISS AT THIS POINT-BLANK RANGE, YOU FOOL!

THIS IS YOUR FINISH, GREEN LANTERN!

IS THIS THEN THE FINAL END OF OUR EMERALD-CLAD HERO? FOR THE GRIPPING ANSWER SEE *PART TWO* ON THE NEXT PAGE FOLLOWING!

10

The STRANGE TRIAL of GREEN LANTERN! PART 2

SOMETHING--HAS GRIPPED ME-- YANKING ME ASIDE JUST AS SINESTRO'S DEADLY RAY WAS ABOUT TO DESTROY ME!

AND SIMULTANEOUSLY INTO THE CHAMBER POURS AN INTREPID GREEN-SUITED BAND...

M-MY FELLOW GREEN LANTERNS!?

YES! WE SUSPECTED THAT SINESTRO MIGHT BE BEHIND YOUR EXTRAORDINARY BE- HAVIOR AT YOUR TRIAL, GREEN LANTERN OF EARTH! SO A POSSE OF US FOLLOWED YOU HERE--

--AND ARRIVED IN TIME TO HEAR EVERYTHING!

YOUR EVIL GENIUS HAS SUCCEEDED IN BRINGING ABOUT ONLY YOUR OWN DESTRUCTION, SINESTRO! FOR NOT EVEN YOU--AND YOUR EVIL POWERS--CAN WITHSTAND THE COMBINED MIGHT OF OUR POWER BEAMS!

THROW DOWN YOUR POWER RING! SURRENDER AT ONCE OR FACE THE CONSEQUENCES!

AND WE'RE GIVING YOU ONE SECOND TO MAKE UP YOUR MIND!

THEN, TO THE AMAZEMENT OF ALL, THE ULTIMATE IN EVIL BURSTS INTO GALES OF LAUGHTER...

HA HO HA HO HA... YOU FOOLS! IT IS CLEAR THAT YOU STILL DO NOT APPRECIATE THE DEPTHS OF MY SINISTER BRAIN! I FIGURED YOU MIGHT GUESS THE TRUTH AT THE TRIAL--AND I MADE PROVISION FOR IT!

WHAT YOU SEE BEFORE YOU IS NOT *SINESTRO* IN PERSON--BUT MERELY A NON-CORPOREAL DUPLICATE OF MYSELF--OPERATED BY REMOTE CONTROL!

FIRE AWAY WITH YOUR *POWER BEAMS*--AND YOU'LL SEE FOR YOURSELVES!

AS BOLTS OF FIERY GREEN ENERGY LICK OUT AT THE MOCKING FIGURE...

HE--HE'S GONE!

THEN IT *WAS* A PROJECTION! IT DISAPPEARED LIKE SOMEONE *TURNING OFF A LIGHT!*

POP!

AND AT THE SAME MOMENT...

THE DOOR HAS SLAMMED SHUT!

A YELLOW DOOR!

CLICK!

GRIMLY, THE ASSEMBLED *HEROES* OF THE COSMOS STARE ABOUT THEM...

EVERY INCH OF THIS CHAMBER IS *YELLOW!*

AND OUR MYSTIC BEAMS HAVE *NO* POWER OVER ANYTHING YELLOW!*

WE CAME HERE TO TRAP SINESTRO-- ONLY TO FIND HE'S *TRAPPED US!*

HA! HA HO!

*Editor's Note: DUE TO A *NECESSARY* IMPURITY IN THE UNIQUE MATERIAL FROM WHICH THE *GREEN LANTERNS'* POWER BATTERIES ARE MADE, THEIR RINGS HAVE NO EFFECT ON ANY-THING YELLOW!

12

IN THAT DREAD-FUL MOMENT, THE ASSEMBLED GREEN LANTERNS ARE ESPECIALLY AWARE OF ONE OF THEIR MEMBERS...

GREEN LANTERN OF EARTH, OUR SITUATION IS CRITICAL! BUT IF THIS DOES TURN OUT TO BE OUR LAST FIGHT, WE WANT YOU ALONGSIDE US--SHOULDER TO SHOULDER--WITH ALL YOUR SUPER-POWERS BACK AND YOUR RING FULLY CHARGED!

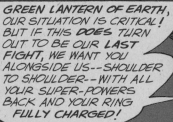

WE ONLY TOOK THEM FROM YOU AS A RUSE-- IN ORDER TO FOLLOW YOU AND GET TO THE BOTTOM OF THIS! NOW YOU ARE ONE OF US AGAIN!

THANK YOU, FELLOW MEMBERS!! I--

BUT BEFORE THE NEWLY RESTORED GL CAN GIVE VENT TO THE HEARTFELT JOY HE FEELS AT GETTING BACK HIS HIGH RANK AND POWERS, TERROR STRIKES...

GREAT GUARDIANS! THAT GAS-- POURING IN ON US!

OUR RINGS CAN'T AFFECT IT--IT'S A YELLOWISH GAS!

THE FAINT WHIFF OF IT COMING TO MY NOSTRILS TELLS ME THAT IT'S CHLORINE-- A DEADLY POISONOUS GAS!

AS THE GREEN-CLAD BAND RETREATS TO THE FURTHEST POINT IT CAN IN THE DOME, AWAY FROM THE BILLOWING FUMES...

WE'VE ONLY GOT A FEW MINUTES BEFORE THAT GAS FILLS THIS CHAMBER-- AND OVERWHELMS US!

IF ONLY THERE WERE SOME-THING WE COULD DO!

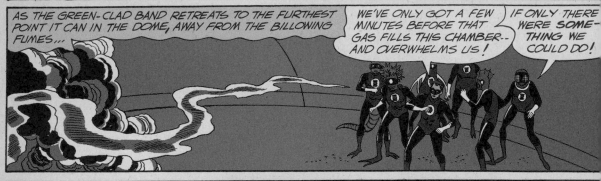

THERE IS! CHEMICALLY, CHLORINE CAN BE TURNED INTO HYDROGEN CHLORIDE, A COLORLESS GAS -- AND THEN-- BY THE ADDITION OF WATER, INTO COLORLESS HYDROCHLORIC ACID!

WATER? BUT--

WHERE CAN WE GET THAT? THERE IS NO WATER HERE!

ONLY ONE POSSIBLE WAY! THE BREATH OF EARTH-PEOPLE CONTAINS **WATER VAPOR!** IF I CAN USE MY RING TO EXTRACT THE WATER FROM MY BREATH AND SHOOT THE **HYDROGEN** ELEMENT AT THAT GAS...

I SHOULD BE ABLE TO TURN IT INTO **HYDROGEN CHLORIDE-- HCL**--SO THAT WE CAN HANDLE IT!

QUICK! ALL OF US--AROUND HIM! WE MUST KEEP THE YELLOW GAS AWAY FROM HIM AS LONG AS WE CAN-- OTHERWISE HIS **POWER RING** WON'T WORK!

THEN, WHILE HIS FELLOW **GREEN LANTERNS** RESORT TO THEIR **ONLY MEANS** OF KEEPING AWAY THE FATAL **CHLORINE**, GL OF **EARTH** CARRIES OUT HIS SCHEME WITH FEVERISH HASTE...

OKAY SO FAR! I'VE GOT A **FINE SPRAY** OF WATER NOW WHICH MY **POWER RING** IS EXTRACTING FROM MY OWN BREATH-- AND I'M READY TO SHOOT IT AT THE GAS! BUT-- WILL MY **IDEA** WORK!?

14

THEN...

PERFECT! THE WATER SPRAY IS TAKING AWAY THE YELLOW COLOR OF THE GAS, *GREEN LANTERN OF EARTH!* YOUR CHEMICAL ACTION IS CONVERTING IT INTO HYDROGEN CHLORIDE!

AS THE GRIMLY DETERMINED *CRUSADER* FOLLOWS UP HIS ADVANTAGE...

NOW THAT I'VE TURNED THE CHLORINE INTO AN *ACID*--I CAN USE ITS *CORROSIVE* EFFECT BY HURLING IT VIA MY *POWER BEAM* AT THAT YELLOW WALL! IT SHOULD "EAT" A WAY OUT OF HERE!!

QUICKLY, THE *CORROSIVE ACID* EFFECT FORMS A LARGE JAGGED APERTURE...

YOU'VE DONE IT, *GREEN LANTERN OF EARTH!* WE CAN GET OUT OF HERE NOW--THROUGH THAT OPENING YOU'VE MADE!

COME ON--THERE'S NOT A MOMENT TO WASTE!

AND INSTANTS AFTERWARD, AIDED BY THEIR *POWER RINGS*, THE AROUSED GREEN LANTERNS HAVE ROOTED OUT AND CORNERED THEIR LONE MALEVOLENT FOE!

AT LAST! WE'VE CAPTURED SINESTRO!

OUR *POWER BEAMS* HAVE MADE HIM HELPLESS!

UHHH!

WE HAVE WON, FELLOW *GREEN LANTERNS!* AND SINCE OUR CODE FORBIDS DESTROYING THIS EVIL CREATURE, I HAVE A SUGGESTION TO MAKE ON HOW TO DEAL WITH HIM--SO THAT HE WILL *NEVER* TROUBLE US AGAIN!

15

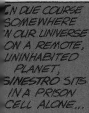

IN DUE COURSE SOMEWHERE IN OUR UNIVERSE, ON A REMOTE, UNINHABITED PLANET, SINESTRO SITS IN A PRISON CELL ALONE...

THERE IS *NO POSSIBLE WAY TO ESCAPE, SINESTRO!* YOU MUST STAY HERE! THERE IS *NO POSSIBLE WAY TO ESCAPE...*

ELSEWHERE ON THE SAME PLANET, THE BAND OF GREEN LANTERNS PREPARES TO DISPERSE AND RETURN TO THEIR SEPARATE WORLDS...

PLACING *SINESTRO* UNDER THE INFLUENCE OF HIS OWN MIND—CONTROL DEVICE WAS A MASTER STROKE, GREEN LANTERN! WE HAVE POWERED THE DEVICE WITH OUR *POWER BEAMS* AND IT WILL NEVER RUN DOWN!

YES--AND UNDER ITS EFFECT IT WILL BE *IMPOSSIBLE* FOR SINESTRO'S BRAIN TO WORK OUT AN ESCAPE! OUR CONGRATULATIONS, *GREEN LANTERN OF EARTH* -- AND FAREWELL!

FAREWELL, FELLOW GREEN LANTERNS-- TILL WE MEET AGAIN!

THUS DO THE GREEN GLADIATORS OF THE COSMOS DEPART, LEAVING BEHIND THEM A FORLORN FIGURE SEEMINGLY FOREVER DOOMED TO HIS LONELY CELL...

YOU MUST STAY HERE! THERE IS NO POSSIBLE WAY TO ESCAPE!

The End

16

BUT IS THIS *REALLY* THE END OF *SINESTRO?* WE ADVISE YOU NOT TO BET ON IT! FOR HIS INFINITELY EVIL BRAIN MAY *STILL* FIND A WAY OUT OF CAPTIVITY AND BACK INTO ACTION AGAINST HIS FOES, THE MIGHTY *GREEN LANTERNS!* TO PLAY SAFE, READER, KEEP YOUR EYE ON FUTURE ISSUES OF THIS MAGAZINE!

GREEN LANTERN

MY IDOL GREEN LANTERN IS FIGHTING THOSE CROOKS-- BUT HE HASN'T GOT HIS *POWER RING!* I HAVE IT ON MY FINGER--AND I MUST FIND A WAY OF GETTING IT TO HIM-- AT ONCE-- !!

ON A GAY AND SUNNY AFTERNOON HAL JORDAN, ACE TEST PILOT, MADE A GRIM DISCOVERY--THAT HE HAD LOST THE MIGHTY POWER RING OF HIS ALTER EGO, GREEN LANTERN! FORTUNATELY THE PRECIOUS RING HAD NOT FALLEN INTO EVIL HANDS-- YET PERIL AND DANGER MOUNTED FAST WHEN THE EMERALD CRUSADER FOLLOWED ...

The TRAIL OF THE MISSING POWER RING!

IN A WEEK-END HOLIDAY MOOD, HAL [GREEN LANTERN] JORDAN TOOLS ACROSS COAST CITY...

IT WAS NICE OF *PIEFACE* AND HIS BRIDE *TERGA* TO INVITE CAROL AND ME TO DINNER TODAY! I IMAGINE WE'LL BE THEIR FIRST GUESTS SINCE THEIR MARRIAGE LAST WEEK-- WHERE I WAS BEST MAN!

I'VE GOT TO GET CAROL A CORSAGE! THAT WILL REMIND HER THAT I STILL HAVE HOPES OF *HER* MARRYING *ME* ONE OF THESE DAYS! HERE'S A FLORIST'S SHOP NOW...

FLORIST

HJ-28

TEN MINUTES LATER WHEN THE ACE TEST PILOT EMERGES FROM THE STORE...

IN BRIGHTEST DAY, IN BLACKEST NIGHT, NO EVIL SHALL ESCAPE MY SIGHT...

GREAT SCOTT!?

YOU CROOKS HAVEN'T A CHANCE! I'M USING MY *POWER BEAM* TO CAPTURE YOU--!

THAT RING-- IT LOOKS JUST LIKE MY *POWER RING!* BUT OF COURSE IT'S NOT REALLY...

...AND I THINK I UNDERSTAND! SOME MANUFACTURER TRYING TO CASH IN ON *GREEN LANTERN'S* REPUTATION HAS TAKEN TO MAKING *TOY POWER RINGS!* I'VE BEEN HALF EXPECTING SOMETHING LIKE THAT--

AND I SUPPOSE I SHOULDN'T COMPLAIN--SINCE IT'S ONE MORE SIGN OF *GREEN LANTERN'S* AMAZING AND GROWING POPULARITY! BUT I'VE GOT TO HUSTLE OR I'LL BE LATE PICKING UP CAROL...

2

AFTER A GAY AND FESTIVE REPAST AT THE THOMAS (*PIEFACE*) KALMAKUS...

TERGA AND I WILL WASH-- BUT YOU TWO WILL DRY! FAIR ENOUGH?

IT'S A DEAL, CAROL! THAT DINNER WAS WORTH IT!

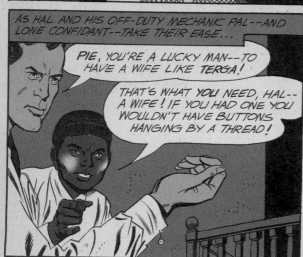

AS HAL AND HIS OFF-DUTY MECHANIC PAL--AND LONE CONFIDANT--TAKE THEIR EASE...

PIE, YOU'RE A LUCKY MAN--TO HAVE A WIFE LIKE TERGA!

THAT'S WHAT *YOU* NEED, HAL-- A WIFE! IF YOU HAD ONE YOU WOULDN'T HAVE BUTTONS HANGING BY A THREAD!

YOUR WIFE WOULD DARN AND SEW FOR YOU-- TAKE CARE OF YOU!

I GUESS YOU'RE RIGHT! I'M GETTING A BIT SEEDY! WHY, LOOK...

...I'M EVEN GETTING HOLES IN MY POCKETS! I DIDN'T REALIZE ... UHHH! GREAT JUMPING JUPITER!

HAL--WHAT'S THE MATTER?

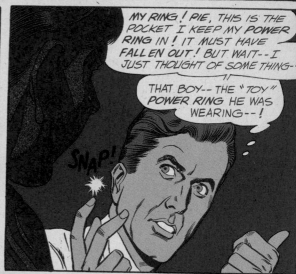

MY RING! PIE, THIS IS THE POCKET I KEEP MY POWER RING IN! IT MUST HAVE FALLEN OUT! BUT WAIT--I JUST THOUGHT OF SOMETHING--

THAT BOY-- THE "TOY" POWER RING HE WAS WEARING--!

SNAP!

INSTANTLY, THE ACE TEST PILOT ACTS ON THIS THOUGHT...

PIE, I'VE NO TIME TO EXPLAIN! COVER ME WITH THE GIRLS-- I'LL BE BACK AS SOON AS I CAN! I'VE GOT TO FIND MY RING--!

OKAY, HAL! I'LL THINK UP SOME EXCUSE FOR YOUR ABSENCE-- DON'T WORRY!

3

MEANWHILE, IN A QUARRY, ON THE OUTSKIRTS OF THE CITY, DESERTED OVER THE WEEK-END...

AW, WE'RE GOING HOME, BILLY! *YOU* ALWAYS WANT TO BE GREEN LANTERN!

WELL, I'VE GOT THE RING!

AFTER BILLY TAYLOR HAS BEEN LEFT ALONE BY HIS PLAYMATES...

GOLLY! I'M BEGINNING TO THINK THIS REALLY IS GREEN LANTERN'S POWER RING! I--I CAN MAKE A SORT OF GREEN BEAM SHOOT OUT OF IT--!!

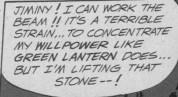

IN EXCITEMENT THE BOY PROPELS THE MYSTIC RAY AT A HANDY OBJECT...

JIMINY! I CAN WORK THE BEAM!! IT'S A TERRIBLE STRAIN...TO CONCENTRATE MY WILLPOWER LIKE GREEN LANTERN DOES...BUT I'M LIFTING THAT STONE--!

I CAN HOLD IT OVER MY HEAD!! I CAN MAKE IT STAY UP THERE!

BUT I GUESS--I OUGHT TO HAND THIS RING OVER TO THE POLICE SO THEY CAN RETURN IT TO GREEN LANTERN! HE MAY NEED IT-- I MUST SEE THAT HE GETS IT BACK AT ONCE!

BUT THE THRILL OF WEARING THE RING TEMPTS THE LAD TO KEEP IT ON A MOMENT LONGER...

GOLLY GEE! NOW I KNOW WHAT GREEN LANTERN HIMSELF FEELS LIKE! IT'S THE GREATEST FEELING IN THE WORLD TO HAVE POWER OVER THIS MAGIC BEAM!

4

BUT THEN, AS WILL SOMETIMES HAPPEN TO THOSE WHO ARE SO CARRIED AWAY, THEY DON'T LOOK WHERE THEY ARE STEPPING...

Uhh--FALLING INTO THIS PIT!

AND THE NEXT MOMENT...

I CAN'T GET OUT! MY LEG IS HURT... AND I CAN HARDLY MOVE! BUT MAYBE... Gasp

COME ON, BANDY! LET'S MOVE!

NO USE! I CAN'T WORK THE RING TO FREE MYSELF EITHER! I--I DON'T HAVE ENOUGH STRENGTH... NOT ENOUGH WILLPOWER...!

SOON, INSIDE THE QUARRY OFFICE BUILDING...

IT WAS A CINCH GETTING RID OF THE WATCH-GUARD FOR THIS QUARRY OFFICE! THERE'S THE SAFE, BANDY!

YEAH--AND I'VE GOT THE CAN OPENER!

MEANWHILE...

THE BIGGER FELLOW WE WERE PLAYING WITH? I GUESS YOU MEAN BILLY, MISTER! WE LEFT HIM AT THE QUARRY--

THE QUARRY? WHERE'S THAT?

ACROSS TOWN! WE PLAY THERE WHEN THERE'S NOBODY WORKING!

THANKS, SON, I'LL FIND IT!

AND SHORTLY...

BURGLARS--AND THEY'RE ROBBING THE SAFE!

LET'S HIKE, RALPH! WE'VE CLEANED IT OUT!

AT ONCE, ALMOST BY REFLEX ACTION, THE YOUNG TEST PILOT SWITCHES TO HIS FAMED ALTER EGO, THE EMERALD GLADIATOR!

EVEN THOUGH I HAVEN'T ANY RING I'M STILL GREEN LANTERN -- AND I'VE GOT TO STOP THOSE CROOKS AT ALL COSTS!

THEN...

G-GREEN LANTERN!?

HOW DID HE GET HERE!?

AS THE AROUSED CRUSADER PILES INTO A FOE...

USING HIS FISTS AGAINST US?!

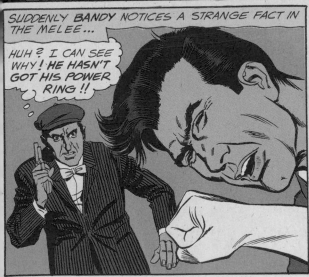

SUDDENLY BANDY NOTICES A STRANGE FACT IN THE MELEE...

HUH? I CAN SEE WHY! HE HASN'T GOT HIS POWER RING!!

AT THAT MOMENT, BELOW IN THE PIT, SMALL EARS HAVE OVERHEARD ALL...

GOLLY GEE! MY IDOL GREEN LANTERN IS FIGHTING CROOKS UP THERE, BUT HE CAN'T USE HIS RING AGAINST THEM BECAUSE... I HAVE IT ON!

6

AT HIM, RALPH! WE DON'T HAVE TO BE AFRAID OF HIM *WITHOUT HIS RING!*

I--I'VE GOT TO DO SOMETHING TO HELP GREEN LANTERN!

IF I COULD SHOOT THE *GREEN BEAM* UP...IT COULD HANDLE THOSE CROOKS! BUT I CAN'T DO IT... I'M TOO WEAK...! AND I CERTAINLY CAN'T *THROW* THE RING UP TO *GREEN LANTERN...*

...BECAUSE I... I CAN HARDLY MOVE! BUT WAIT A SECOND... I JUST THOUGHT OF SOMETHING...!

WE'RE OVERPOWERIN' HIM, BANDY!

...MAYBE...MAYBE I CAN USE MY *WILLPOWER* TO SHOOT THE RING ITSELF UP TO HIM! GOT TO TRY IT... I'VE GOT TO TRY IT!

CONCENTRATING AS HARD AS HE CAN, YOUNG BILLY BENDS EVERY OUNCE OF HIS STRENGTH TO THE TASK...

I MUST SHUT OUT EVERYTHING ELSE FROM MY MIND...I MUST MAKE THE RING SHOOT UPWARD...

IT...IT'S MOVING! GOT TO...TRY HARDER... HARDER...!

IT'S OFF MY FINGER...! IT'S STARTING TO GO...!

7

THE NEXT MOMENT, NEAR THE PIT...

EH?

HIT HIM, BANDY! CONK HIM OUT!

HERE GOES--

I MANAGED TO TWIST OUT OF THE WAY OF THAT BLOW...I MAY NOT BE SO LUCKY NEXT TIME...THAT RING-- IT LOOKS LIKE MY POWER RING--!

WITH A CONVULSIVE EFFORT, THE DOWNED GLADIATOR MANAGES TO UPSET THE FOES ATOP HIM...

GRAB HIM, RALPH--!

GOT TO GET TO THAT RING--!

THIS IS MY POWER RING! IT HAS TO BE!

I AIN'T GONNA WASTE ANY MORE TIME ON HIM, RALPH! I'M GONNA BLAST HIM--BUT GOOD!

BUT THE NEXT INSTANT EVEN BEFORE THE THUG CAN FIRE...

ANY BLASTING DONE AROUND HERE--I'M GOING TO DO IT!

CAAAA!

BRINGING HIS NEWLY RECOVERED POWER RING INTO PLAY TO FORM A GIANT FIRE HOSE, THE EMERALD GLADIATOR PLAYS A HEAVY, SUPER-SWIFT STREAM OF WATER ON HIS TWO ASSAILANTS!

8

AND LATER WITH ALL THE "FIRE" DOUSED OUT OF THE THIEVES...

WH-WHAT HAPPENED TO US, BANDY?

I'LL JUST USE MY GREEN BEAM TO CAGE THOSE HOODLUMS UNTIL I CAN TURN THEM IN TO THE POLICE...

...BUT MEANWHILE I'VE GOT TO HAVE A LOOK DOWN INTO THIS QUARRY HOLE WHERE THE RING CAME FROM... AND I HAVE AN IDEA WHAT I'LL FIND DOWN THERE...!

I THOUGHT SO! IT'S THE BOY NAMED BILLY--THE ONE I SAW PLAYING WITH MY RING NEAR THE FLORIST'S SHOP--WHERE IT MUST HAVE SLIPPED THROUGH THE HOLE IN MY POCKET! BUT HE SEEMS HURT...!

WITH INFINITE CARE, THE GREEN-CLAD CRUSADER EMPLOYS HIS RING TO FREE THE LAD AND RAISE HIM TO THE SURFACE...

GEE! THE WAY GREEN LANTERN USES HIS RING--IT'S TERRIFIC!

YOU ALL RIGHT, BILLY?

YES, I AM, GREEN LANTERN--THANKS TO YOU!

YOU MEAN I'M ALL RIGHT-- THANKS TO YOU, BILLY! YOU SURE THOUGHT QUICKLY--THE WAY YOU "POWERED" THAT RING TO ME! AND IN RETURN I'M GOING TO GIVE YOU A SOUVENIR TO REMEMBER THIS OCCASION!

ONCE MORE THE MIGHTY POWER RING OPERATES, THIS TIME TO FASHION A TOY DUPLICATE OF ITSELF!

A--A SPECIAL RING LIKE YOURS FOR ME? WOW--EE! DO YOU THINK I REALLY DESERVE SUCH A WONDERFUL PRESENT?

YOU SURE DO, BILLY! AND HAVE A GOOD TIME PLAYING WITH IT!

THIS EXPERIENCE HAS TAUGHT ME THAT AS HAL JORDAN I MUST NEVER AGAIN KEEP THE POWER RING IN MY POCKET! FROM NOW ON, I'LL ALWAYS WEAR IT ON MY FINGER--BUT IT WILL BE CONCEALED FROM VIEW BY AN INVISIBILITY SHIELD WHEN I WEAR IT AS HAL!

Shortly, with the crooks in custody, Hal Jordan reappears at Pieface's apartment house...

I waited down here to meet you, Hal--because I wanted to tip you off to the excuse I made up for you! I said you'd lost your wallet and went out to find it!

Good enough! And I did find what I went out for, Pie...

...So now we can all settle down to a pleasant afternoon... while I use the opportunity to try and convince Carol that she loves me enough to marry me!

Good idea, Hal! Terga and I will-- er--give you two time to be alone--!

But upstairs, not long afterward...

Pieface has the most marvelous collection of Green Lantern scrapbooks! I could spend days going through them--!

Great days! She's hardly aware of me anymore...

All she can think of is Green Lantern!! (Sigh!) Once again my alter ego has come between me and my lady love!

He's wonderful..!

The End

10

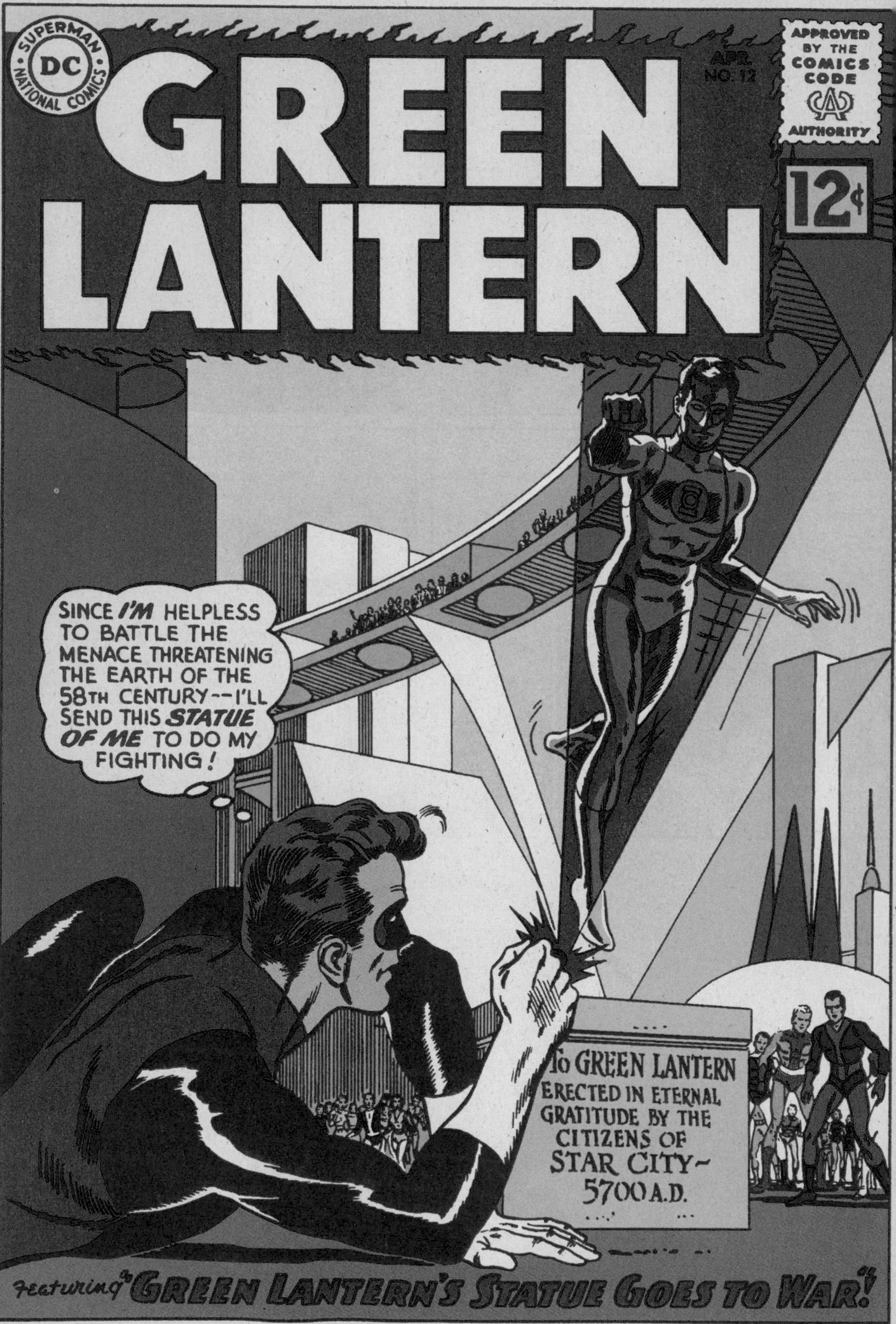

SUPERMAN DC NATIONAL COMICS
GREEN LANTERN
APR. NO. 12
APPROVED BY THE COMICS CODE AUTHORITY
12¢
SINCE I'M HELPLESS TO BATTLE THE MENACE THREATENING THE EARTH OF THE 58TH CENTURY--I'LL SEND THIS STATUE OF ME TO DO MY FIGHTING!
TO GREEN LANTERN ERECTED IN ETERNAL GRATITUDE BY THE CITIZENS OF STAR CITY- 5700 A.D.
Featuring "GREEN LANTERN'S STATUE GOES TO WAR!"

GREEN LANTERN

IN THE FAROFF 58th CENTURY, GREEN LANTERN HAD BECOME THE ALL-POWERFUL SOLAR DIRECTOR... AND EVEN RATED A FULL-SIZE STATUE DEDICATED TO HIM IN A CENTRAL SQUARE OF THE CITY! BUT NO ONE--LEAST OF ALL THE EMERALD GLADIATOR--COULD HAVE FORESEEN THAT THIS METALLIC REPLICA OF HIMSELF WOULD ONE DAY BE THE MEANS OF SAVING THE DEMOCRATIC CIVILIZATION OF EARTH!

GREEN LANTERN'S STATUE GOES TO WAR!

MY MAGIC POWERS HAVE DEFEATED GREEN LANTERN--BUT WILL THEY BE ABLE TO OVERCOME THIS STATUE OF HIMSELF THAT GREEN LANTERN HAS SENT AGAINST ME?

IN ACE TEST PILOT HAL JORDAN'S DRESSING ROOM, HIS ALTER EGO GREEN LANTERN NOTICES AN ODD THING...

WHERE DID THIS TINY PIECE OF METAL COME FROM? IT WASN'T THERE WHEN I COMBED MY HAIR A MOMENT AGO...AND IT COULDN'T HAVE DROPPED FROM THE CEILING..!

CURIOUS, THE EMERALD GLADIATOR TRAINS HIS POWER RING ON THE OBJECT...

THIS IS INCREDIBLE! MY POWER BEAM SPECTROSCOPICALLY REVEALS THAT THIS IS AN UNKNOWN METAL -- NEVER BEFORE SEEN ON EARTH!

THE INCIDENT SETS OFF A TRAIN OF THOUGHT IN THE GREEN-CLAD FIGURE...

SOMETIME AGO MY RING MYSTERIOUSLY RAN OUT OF POWER LONG BEFORE ITS 24-HOUR CHARGE SHOULD HAVE BEEN EXHAUSTED!* I COULDN'T EXPLAIN THAT OCCURRENCE THEN...AND I CAN'T EXPLAIN THIS ONE NOW!

WHICH LEADS ME TO WONDER...CAN THERE BE ANY CONNECTION BETWEEN THE TWO EVENTS? I HAVE AN ODD FEELING THAT...SOMETHING IS HAPPENING TO ME THAT I DON'T KNOW ANYTHING ABOUT!

AMAZINGLY, THE KEEN MIND OF THE GREEN-GARBED CRUSADER HAS HIT UPON THE TRUTH! BUT NOT EVEN IN HIS WILDEST IMAGININGS COULD GREEN LANTERN DREAM WHAT LIES BEHIND THAT CHANCE THOUGHT OF HIS! TO EXPLAIN IT...

*Editor's Note: AS REVEALED IN GREEN LANTERN #8, "The CHALLENGE FROM 5700 A.D.!"

..WE MUST TRAVEL 3740 YEARS FORWARD IN TIME TO THE YEAR 5702 WHEN ALL THE SOLAR SYSTEM PLANETS ARE UNDER DOMINION OF THE EARTH...AND ONE MAN, THE SOLAR DIRECTOR IN STAR CITY, WIELDS MORE POWER THAN ANY HUMAN IN HISTORY...

GREEN LANTERN SOLAR DIRECTOR

...THE MAN NAMED GREEN LANTERN...WHOSE CHAIR IS EMPTY...BUT WITH GOOD REASON...

WE MUST REACH INTO THE PAST AGAIN, IONA, TO BRING OUR SOLAR DIRECTOR, GREEN LANTERN, HERE TO OUR ERA AT ONCE!

As DASOR, CHAIRMAN OF THE SOLAR COUNCIL, AND HIS SECRETARY IONA VANE BUSY THEMSELVES WITH THEIR ALL-IMPORTANT TASK...

IT IS TWO YEARS NOW SINCE WE LAST CALLED UPON GREEN LANTERN, IONA--

YES, CHAIRMAN DASOR--IT WAS DURING THE INVASION OF THE ZEGORS!

TWO YEARS... AND YET I DON'T THINK THERE'S BEEN A DAY SINCE THAT I HAVEN'T THOUGHT ABOUT GREEN LANTERN! AND NOW-- HOW FAST MY HEART IS BEATING AT THE THOUGHT THAT I WILL SEE HIM AGAIN!

BUT WHILE IONA WAITS BREATHLESSLY, LET US BRIEFLY REVIEW THE CIRCUMSTANCES AND STRANGE CONDITIONS ATTENDANT UPON GREEN LANTERN'S LAST VISIT TO THE FAR FUTURE, THE WORLD OF 5700 A.D. ...

...AND A MEETING OF THE HIGH COUNCIL OF SOLAR DELEGATES SITTING IN SOLAR HALL, STAR CITY, IN A GRAVE EMERGENCY SESSION...

FELLOW SOLARITES*, WE ARE MET IN THIS CRISIS TO CONSIDER A NEW CANDIDATE FOR THE CRUCIAL POST OF SOLAR DIRECTOR! MANY CANDIDATES HAVE BEEN CONSIDERED--

YES! BUT NONE OF THEM WAS EQUAL TO THE JOB!

*Editor's Note: BY 5700 A.D., CENTURIES OF LIVING ON OTHER SOLAR SYSTEM WORLDS HAVE CHANGED THE COLONIZING EARTHLINGS ACCORDING TO THE CLIMATIC CONDITIONS OF THEIR NEW HOMES!

BEFORE I REVEAL THE LATEST CANDIDATE, I MUST REMIND YOU THAT NOT LONG AGO OUR SCIENCE DEVELOPED THE ABILITY TO PEER AT WILL INTO THE PAST-- IN EFFECT, TO VIEW HISTORY AS IT HAPPENS-- BY THE INVENTION OF THE TIMESCOPE!

NOW BY LINKING UP A COMMON MATTER TELEPORTER TO THE TIMESCOPE WE ARE ABLE TO BRING ANYTHING-- OR ANYONE-- WE CHOOSE FROM THE PAST INTO THE PRESENT! IN THE COURSE OF OUR RESEARCHES INTO THE PAST...

"...MY SECRETARY IONA VANE AND I CAME ACROSS A TRULY AMAZING INDIVIDUAL, IN THE FARAWAY TWENTIETH CENTURY, NAMED GREEN LANTERN..."

HE IS ABSOLUTELY FEARLESS!

A CHAMPION OF CHAMPIONS!

3

SINCE WE HAVE NOT BEEN ABLE TO FIND A GREAT LEADER IN OUR OWN ERA, I PROPOSE THAT WE BRING THIS ANCIENT HERO *GREEN LANTERN* TO OUR TIME AND MAKE HIM OUR *SOLAR DIRECTOR!*

WHAT AN ASTONISHING PROPOSAL!

AFTER THE MATTER WAS WEIGHED CAREFULLY AND EVERY FACET OF *GREEN LANTERN'S* LIFE HAD BEEN EXAMINED...

WE AGREE, CHAIRMAN *DASOR!* YOU HAVE FOUND OUR *SOLAR DIRECTOR!* BUT HURRY-- THERE IS VERY LITTLE TIME--!

EVERYTHING IS READY, FELLOW SOLARITES-- EXCEPT FOR ONE PROBLEM...

TO TRAVEL IN TIME CAUSES AN INDIVIDUAL'S MEMORY TO BE COMPLETELY WIPED OUT! IF *GREEN LANTERN* CAME HERE WITHOUT HIS "LIFE-HISTORY" HE WOULD BE DAZED--OF LITTLE USE TO US!

BUT *HOW* CAN SUCH AN OBSTACLE BE OVERCOME?

SIMPLY! MISS VANE HAS PRE-PARED A FICTITIOUS PERSONAL HISTORY FOR *GREEN LANTERN!* HE WILL *BELIEVE* THAT HE IS A FAMOUS *SPACE-EXPLORER* OF OUR ERA NAMED *POL MANNING* WHO HAS JUST BEEN SUMMONED BACK TO EARTH TO DEAL WITH THE DREADFUL MENACE OF THE *ZEGORS!* BUT WAIT--!

THERE IS ONE THING YOU HAVE OMITTED, MISS VANE! A YOUNG MAN LIKE *GREEN LANTERN* WOULD CERTAINLY HAVE A *ROMANTIC INTEREST!*... AND SINCE *YOU* ARE UNMARRIED AND UNATTACHED, *IONA*, IT OCCURS TO ME THAT *YOU* CAN BE HIS ROMANTIC INTEREST!

M-ME!?

AS MEMORIES OF THAT PRE-VIOUS TIME FLOOD OVER *IONA* NOW...

I THOUGHT IT WAS JUST GOING TO BE A GAME FOR ME TO PLAY! I DIDN'T REALIZE IT WOULD BE *FOR KEEPS*--AS FAR AS I'M CONCERNED!

READY, *IONA!* I'M STARTING THE TELEPORTER..!

AND NOW LET US RETURN TO THE MOMENT *BEFORE* GREEN LANTERN FOUND THE STRANGE PIECE OF METAL IN HIS HAIR...

I'D GIVE A LOT TO FIGURE OUT WHY MY *POWER RING* MYSTERIOUSLY RAN OUT OF CHARGE A WHILE AGO! I--eh? A QUEER TREMBLING... LIKE A SUDDEN FEVER... ALL OVER ME--!

AN INSTANT LATER, BY THE INCREDIBLE MAGIC OF FIFTY--EIGHTH CENTURY SCIENCE...

WE'VE BROUGHT HIM BACK, IONA! AND AS ALWAYS THIS MOMENT IS CRITICAL! IT WILL NOT BE NECESSARY TO FEED HIS *PSEUDO-HISTORY* INTO GREEN LANTERN'S MIND AGAIN-- AUTOMATICALLY, NOW THAT HE IS IN OUR ERA, THAT PART OF HIS MIND WILL TAKE OVER...

...JUST AS HIS IDENTITY AS *HAL JORDAN* IN THE TWENTIETH CENTURY IS AUTOMATICALLY ERASED FROM HIS MIND DURING HIS STAY WITH US! BUT STILL THE *PAST TWO YEARS* HERE MUST BE ACCOUNTED FOR, TO PREVENT HIM FROM BEING DAZED OR UNCERTAIN!

IN THE SPLIT-SECONDS BEFORE THE MISTS DISSOLVE FROM IN FRONT OF GREEN LANTERN'S EYES, AN ELECTRONIC DEVICE OPERATES SILENTLY.

DURING THE PAST TWO YEARS, *GREEN LANTERN*, YOU HAVE BEEN ON A LONE DEEP-SPACE EXPLORATION IN THE PERSON OF YOUR ALTER EGO *POL MANNING!* WHILE YOU WERE AWAY CHAIRMAN *DASOR* AND *IONA* ACTED IN YOUR BEHALF HERE IN *STAR CITY*...

THEY ISSUED ORDERS AND RELEASED PROCLAMATIONS UNDER YOUR SIGNATURE AS *SOLAR DIRECTOR!* AND YOU KEPT IN CONSTANT TOUCH WITH THEM BY SPACE-RADIO! BUT THIS WEEK YOU HEARD THE ALARMING NEWS OF THE *REVOLT* OF THE EARTH GENERALS...

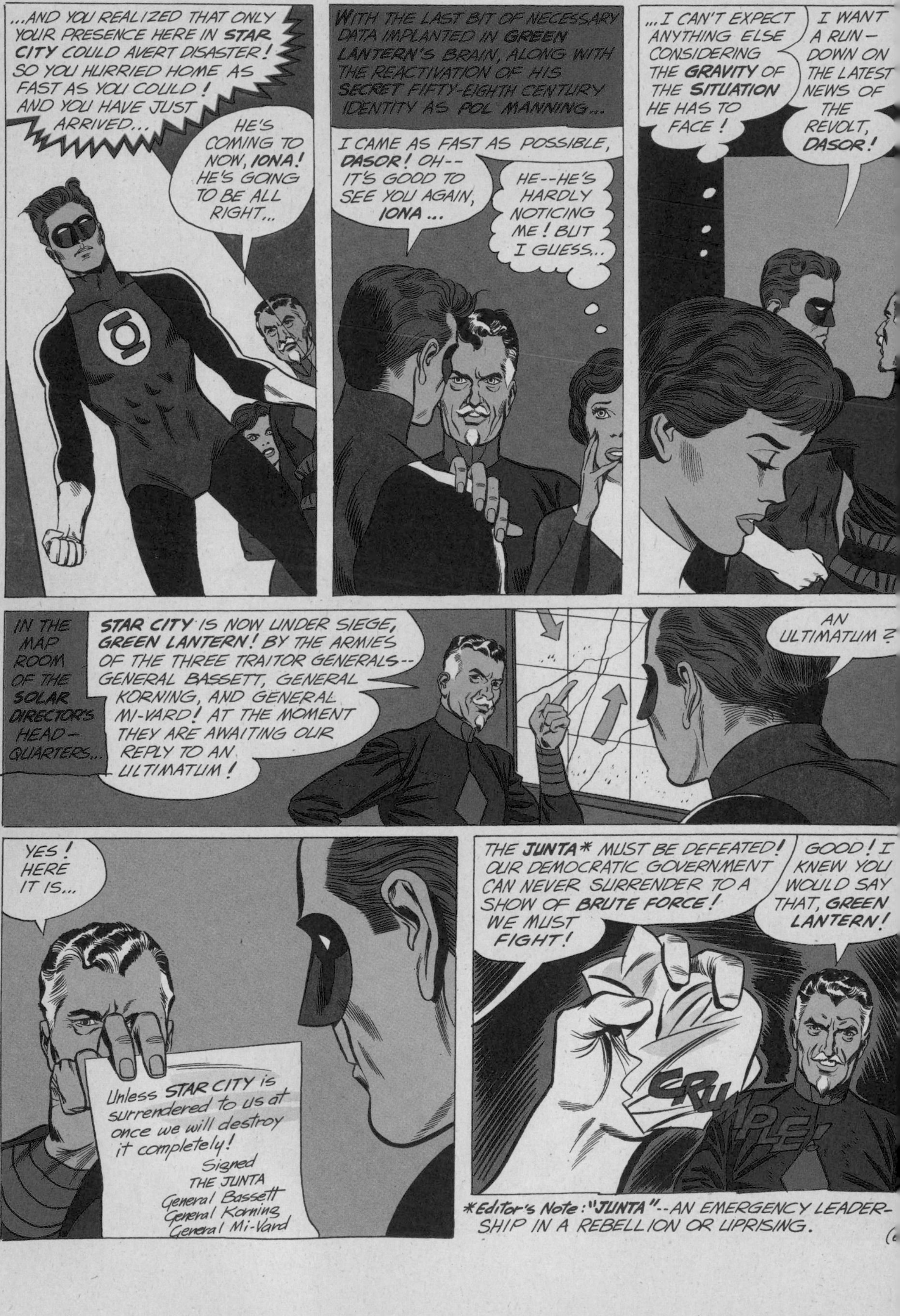
...AND YOU REALIZED THAT ONLY YOUR PRESENCE HERE IN STAR CITY COULD AVERT DISASTER! SO YOU HURRIED HOME AS FAST AS YOU COULD! AND YOU HAVE JUST ARRIVED...
HE'S COMING TO NOW, IONA! HE'S GOING TO BE ALL RIGHT...
WITH THE LAST BIT OF NECESSARY DATA IMPLANTED IN GREEN LANTERN'S BRAIN, ALONG WITH THE REACTIVATION OF HIS SECRET FIFTY-EIGHTH CENTURY IDENTITY AS POL MANNING...
I CAME AS FAST AS POSSIBLE, DASOR! OH-- IT'S GOOD TO SEE YOU AGAIN, IONA...
HE--HE'S HARDLY NOTICING ME! BUT I GUESS...
...I CAN'T EXPECT ANYTHING ELSE CONSIDERING THE GRAVITY OF THE SITUATION HE HAS TO FACE!
I WANT A RUN-DOWN ON THE LATEST NEWS OF THE REVOLT, DASOR!
IN THE MAP ROOM OF THE SOLAR DIRECTOR'S HEAD-QUARTERS...
STAR CITY IS NOW UNDER SIEGE, GREEN LANTERN! BY THE ARMIES OF THE THREE TRAITOR GENERALS-- GENERAL BASSETT, GENERAL KORNING, AND GENERAL MI-VARD! AT THE MOMENT THEY ARE AWAITING OUR REPLY TO AN ULTIMATUM!
AN ULTIMATUM?
YES! HERE IT IS...
Unless STAR CITY is surrendered to us at once we will destroy it completely! Signed THE JUNTA General Bassett General Korning General Mi-Vard
THE JUNTA* MUST BE DEFEATED! OUR DEMOCRATIC GOVERNMENT CAN NEVER SURRENDER TO A SHOW OF BRUTE FORCE! WE MUST FIGHT!
GOOD! I KNEW YOU WOULD SAY THAT, GREEN LANTERN!
CRUMPLE!
*Editor's Note: "JUNTA"--AN EMERGENCY LEADERSHIP IN A REBELLION OR UPRISING.

WITH A TERRIFIC BLAZE OF ENERGY, THE GREEN-CLAD SOLAR DIRECTOR SWINGS INTO ACTION, AS IF HE HAD NEVER BEEN AWAY FROM HIS DESK...

HAVE ALL ABLE-BODIED MEN REPORT TO THEIR SPACE-RAID STATIONS FOR MILITARY DUTY!

ALL AVAILABLE ARMS IN OUR ARSENALS WILL BE PASSED OUT TO CITIZENS WHO WANT TO HELP DEFEND THE CITY!

THE LOYAL SPACE-LEGION FROM PLUTO IS ON ITS WAY, MR. SOLAR DIRECTOR!

HAVE THEM ATTACK THE ENEMY WITHOUT DELAY!

HE'S INSPIRING!

I ADMIT I WAS GETTING DISCOURAGED, IONA, BUT NOW I'M FEELING MUCH BETTER ABOUT OUR CHANCES OF CRUSHING THIS REBELLION -- WITH GREEN LANTERN ON THE JOB!

SOON... THE SPACE-LEGION FROM PLUTO HAS ARRIVED! I'VE GIVEN ORDERS FOR THEM TO ENGAGE GENERAL BASSETT'S FORCES ON THE NORTH -- THE CLOSEST TO THE CITY!

ON THE TELESCREEN AT HEADQUARTERS, A GRIM GROUP VIEWS A THRILLING SIGHT AS THE LOYAL SPACE-TROOPERS FROM PLUTO FLUMMET DOWN ON THE FOE...

THE PLUTO-LEGIONNAIRES ARE FIRING PARALO-PISTOLS! THEY HAVE TO GET WITHIN RANGE TO PARALYZE THE FOE!

THE ENEMY IS SHOOTING NERVE-GUNS -- AND TAKING A HEAVY TOLL OF OUR SOLDIERS!

7

THEN... OUR LEGION IS BEING BEATEN BACK! THEY'RE RETREATING TOWARD THE CITY!

ONLY ONE THING TO DO NOW...!

WHAT?! YOU'RE PERSONALLY GOING TO SEEK OUT THE JUNTA--AND TRY TO SEIZE THEM TO STOP THE REVOLT, GREEN LANTERN?

IT'S OUR ONLY CHANCE, IONA!

AT ONCE, THE SOLAR COUNCIL CHAIRMAN EXPRESS EQUAL DISMAY...

BUT EVEN WITH YOUR MIGHTY POWER RING YOU ARE NOT INVULNER-ABLE, GREEN LANTERN! IN THE ENEMY RANKS YOU MAY MEET DISASTER--LEAVING US LEADERLESS! IT'S A TERRIBLE RISK--

IT'S ONE WE HAVE TO TAKE, DASOR! YOU WILL BE IN CHARGE WHILE I AM GONE!

THE NEXT MOMENT...

NO WORD OF FAREWELL-- AND I--I MAY NEVER SEE HIM AGAIN!

AS THE INTREPID LEADER SPEEDS TOWARD THE BATTLEFIELD, HE PASSES OVER A SINGLE REMINDER OF THE REVERENCE IN WHICH HE IS HELD BY HIS FELLOW CITIZENS...

DASOR TOLD ME ABOUT THIS! THEY'VE ERECTED A STATUE TO ME HERE IN STAR SQUARE!* I MUST CONTINUE TO PROVE MYSELF WORTHY OF SUCH HIGH REGARD!

TO GREEN LANTERN ERECTED IN ETERNAL GRATITUDE BY THE CITIZENS OF STAR CITY 5705

*Editor's Note: TO COMMEMORATE GREEN LANTERN'S HEROIC EFFORTS IN HALTING THE RAVAGES OF THE ZEGORS TWO YEARS BEFORE!

I'VE GOT TO CAPTURE THOSE THREE GENERALS--AND LEARN WHY THEY SUDDENL REBELLED AGAINST SOLAR AUTHORITY!

ACCORDING TO OUR INTELLIGENCE, THE COM BINED HEADQUARTERS OF THE JUNTA IS A FEW MILES NORTH...

REACHING THE WELL-PROTECTED COMMAND POST OF THE JUNTA, THE EMERALD WARRIOR BARRELS HIS WAY IN VIA HIS *POWER RING*-- ONLY TO SET OFF AUTOMATIC WEAPONS, TRIGGERED BY ELECTRIC-EYES, THAT THREATEN TO BLAST HIM INTO ETERNITY!

THERE ARE THE THREE GENERALS! BUT-- THEY'VE GOT THIS PLACE "MINED" WITH GUNS -- SET SECRETLY INTO THE WALLS! AND DESIGNED TO BLAST AN INTRUDER LIKE ME!

IT'S THE *SOLAR DIRECTOR!*

HIS *LIGHTNING-LIKE* REFLEXES WORKING AT TOP SPEED, GREEN LANTERN WARDS OFF THE AUTOMATIC ATTACK...

MY *POWER BEAM* IS DESTROYING THE CONCEALED WEAPONS -- EXPLODING THEM BEFORE THEY CAN HARM ME!

THEN... THE GENERALS HAVE PULLED *NERVE-PISTOLS!* IF ANY OF THOSE RAYS TOUCH ME --!

IN AN INSTANT, THE REBEL OVERLORDS ARE ENCASED IN AN IMPENETRABLE *GREEN PRISON* ALONG WITH THEIR WEAPONS...

THE DEADLY RAYS CAN'T GET THROUGH MY *POWER RING BUBBLE*--AND NEITHER CAN THE GENERALS! NOW TO GET THEM BACK TO HEADQUARTERS-- WHERE I CAN INTERROGATE THEM!

AS THE ONE-MAN *TASK FORCE* RETURNS GRIMLY TO HIS OWN LINES...

WHY SHOULD THESE THREE GENERALS LEAD A REVOLT-- WHEN THEY HAD ALWAYS BEEN *LOYAL* TO THE *SOLAR COUNCIL*? THAT'S WHAT I'VE GOT TO FIND OUT--TO PREVENT ANYTHING LIKE THIS FROM EVER HAPPENING AGAIN!

SOON, THE MIGHTY CRUSADER USES HIS *POWER BEAM* AS A *TRUTH RAY*...

I'LL START WITH GENERAL BASSETT-- HE'S SENIOR TO THE OTHERS! UNDER MY POWER RING HE *MUST* TELL THE *TRUTH*--HE CAN'T HELP HIMSELF!

WHAT MADE YOU RISE AGAINST THE *SOLAR COUNCIL*! EXPLAIN!

I--I DON'T KNOW!

TO GREEN LANTERN'S ASTONISHMENT AS HE QUERIES THE REMAINING PAIR...

·I DON'T KNOW!

I...CAN'T EXPLAIN!

INCREDIBLE! NONE OF THE GENERALS SEEMS ABLE TO SAY *WHY* HE LED THE REVOLT! THIS COULD MEAN THERE'S *SOMETHING* BEHIND THE UPRISING THAT NO ONE SUSPECTS! BUT *WHAT*--?

AT THAT MOMENT IN THE ANTEROOM OUTSIDE...

YES, THE *SOLAR DIRECTOR* IS IN HIS HEADQUARTERS, *ALDEBARAN*! BUT HE MAY BE TOO BUSY TO SEE YOU! I'LL FIND OUT...

PLEASE DO, MISS VANE! IT'S OF THE GREATEST IMPORTANCE TO BOTH OF US!

ALDEBARAN? WHO IS *HE*?

GOODNESS! I FORGOT THAT *GREEN LANTERN* HAS NOT BEEN BRIEFED ON *ALL* THE DETAILS OF OUR FIFTY-EIGHTH CENTURY LIFE!

er--DURING THE LAST TWO YEARS WHILE YOU WERE AWAY FROM *STAR CITY*, GREEN LANTERN...

10

..THIS **FERENC ALDEBARAN** EMERGED AS THE MOST STRIKING FIGURE OF OUR AGE--EXCEPT YOURSELF OF COURSE! HE IS PROBABLY THE **GREATEST** MAGICIAN WHO EVER LIVED!

A MAGICIAN?

YES! HE SAYS HE HAS JUST RETURNED FROM A TOUR-- AND HE ABSOLUTELY **INSISTS** ON SEEING YOU!

WELL...ALL RIGHT! I'LL GIVE HIM A MOMENT TO FIND OUT WHAT HE WANTS!

AND SOON, WITH THE GENERALS IN CUSTODY IN AN ADJOINING CHAMBER..

AS YOU MUST KNOW, MR. **SOLAR DIRECTOR**, MY POWERS ARE NOT INCONSIDERABLE! AND I HAVE COME TO PLACE THEM AT YOUR SERVICE --TO HELP QUELL THIS REBELLION!

Hmmm! SO **THAT'S** IT?

I'M SORRY, **ALDEBARAN**, BUT THERE IS NO PLACE FOR YOU IN THE WAR EFFORT AT THIS TIME! AND NOW IF YOU'LL EXCUSE ME ...

WAIT, PLEASE! EVEN IF I CAN'T HELP AS A SOLDIER I WANT TO DO **SOME-THING** ...

PERHAPS I CAN AMUSE YOU AND RELAX YOUR MIND WITH ONE OR TWO OF MY **FABULOUS TRICKS** -- AND IN THAT WAY HELP THE WAR EFFORT! I KNOW THAT YOUR MIND NOW MUST BE **HEAVY WITH CARE** ...

...EVEN THOUGH YOU HAVE CAPTURED THE **THREE TRAITOR GENERALS**!

A LITTLE TRIFLE, SIR... PICK A CARD...

HE **IS** INSISTENT!

er--JACK OF DIAMONDS.

11

AS THE RENOWNED PRESTIDIGITATOR PERFORMS FOR HIS AUDIENCE OF ONE...

OBSERVE... WITH MY WAND I MERELY TAP THE DECK...

...AND OUT OF THE DECK COMES A CARD!

...THAT GROWS LARGER BEFORE YOUR EYES! LARGER...

...AND NOW IT IS THE SIZE OF A SMALL CARPET! WHAT CARD? NATURALLY THE JACK OF DIAMONDS!

VERY CLEVER, ALDEBARAN...

SUDDENLY, THE MYSTIC POWER BEAM SHOOTS OUT...

...BUT WHILE WE'RE AT IT WHY DON'T WE TURN THE CARD INTO A REAL CARPET--IN FACT, INTO A FLYING CARPET...

!?

...ONE THAT WILL RIDE YOU OUT OF HERE SO I CAN GET BACK TO IMPORTANT THINGS!

UH... HIS MAGIC TRICK TOPPED MINE!

I HAVE AN ODD FEELING ABOUT ALDEBARAN... BUT I CAN'T PUT MY FINGER ON THE REASON FOR IT!

LATER, AS GREEN LANTERN RESUMES QUESTIONING HIS THREE PRIZE CAPTIVES...

I'VE GOT TO GET TO THE ORIGIN OF THE REVOLT!

GENERAL BASSETT, REPEAT YOUR MOVEMENTS DURING THE PAST WEEK!

I MUST TELL THE TRUTH...

SOON AFTER...

...AND THAT IS ALL I REMEMBER...

I BETTER QUESTION THE OTHER TWO GENERALS AGAIN! WHAT BASSETT JUST SAID HAS GIVEN ME A CLUE!

SHORTLY...

I...CAN'T REMEMBER ANYTHING AFTER THAT...

AMAZING! THE LAST THING THE GENERALS CAN RECALL IS A CERTAIN EVENING HERE IN **STAR CITY** EXACTLY SEVEN DAYS AGO...

"...WHEN AT A FESTIVE STATE DINNER **ALDEBARAN** APPEARED TO ENTERTAIN THE ASSEMBLED NOTABLES..."

WATCH MY WAND, PLEASE! WATCH IT **CLOSELY!**

ALDEBARAN AGAIN! THE GENERALS ARE UNABLE TO RECALL *ANYTHING* AFTER THAT MOMENT! IT'S AS IF THEY WERE UNDER A SPELL ALL DURING THE REVOLT! AND--I JUST THOUGHT OF SOMETHING ELSE THAT FITS IN-- SOMETHING **ALDEBARAN** SAID A FEW MINUTES AGO--! HIS WORDS WERE--

"--EVEN THOUGH YOU HAVE CAPTURED THE **THREE TRAITOR GENERALS!**" BUT *HOW* COULD HE HAVE KNOWN *THAT* SINCE I HAVEN'T RELEASED THE NEWS YET TO THE PUBLIC--AND EVEN HERE IN HEADQUARTERS ONLY **IONA** KNOWS ABOUT IT! I'D BETTER CHECK WITH HER...

13.

SOON, IN THE OFFICE OF THE TRUSTED SECRETARY...

NO, GREEN LANTERN-- I SAID NOTHING TO ALDEBARAN ABOUT THE CAPTURED GENERALS!

THAT SETTLES IT! I THINK I'VE FINALLY GOTTEN TO THE BOTTOM OF THIS MYSTERY! TELL ME, IONA-- WHERE DOES ALDEBARAN LIVE?

AFTER GL HAS BEEN GIVEN THE INFORMATION...

I DON'T KNOW WHAT HIS GAME IS, IONA.. BUT I'M CONVINCED ALDEBARAN WAS BEHIND THIS ENTIRE REVOLT!

GREAT TERRA! BE CAREFUL, GREEN LANTERN--

ALDEBARAN COULD BE DANGEROUS-- WITH HIS EXTRA-ORDINARY POWERS!

DON'T WORRY, IONA IF THAT MAGICIAN EVER WANTED TO MATCH HIS POWERS AGAINST MY POWER RING-- HE'S GOING TO GET THE CHANCE NOW!

BUT AT THAT VERY MOMENT IN THE MAGICIAN'S HEAD-QUARTERS...

...HE'S GOING TO GET THE CHANCE NOW...

SO GREEN LANTERN IS COMING AFTER ME! Hmmm! THEN HE MUST HAVE FOUND OUT...

...THAT I SEIZED THE MINDS OF THOSE GENERALS AT THE STATE DINNER-- JUST AS I ATTEMPTED TO SEIZE HIS MIND AT HIS OFFICE WHEN I PERFORMED MY TRICK! BUT BY OUT-TRICKING ME HE ESCAPED MY SPELL! NOW, HOWEVER, I'VE GOT TO HANDLE HIM IN ANOTHER FASHION-- AND QUICKLY!

I'LL USE THE SAME MENTO-RAY THAT I USED TO CONTROL THE BEHAVIOR OF THE GENERALS-- AND BY FOCUSING IT ON GREEN LANTERN ... AND STEPPING UP THE VOLTAGE ...

14

SIMULTANEOUSLY, A TERRIFIC *ENERGY-BLAST* EXPLODES IN THE BRAIN OF THE UNWARY GLADIATOR...

UH!! SOMETHING... KNOCKING ME DOWN! ALMOST... CAUSING ME TO *LOSE* CONSCIOUSNESS...!

AS GREEN LANTERN LIES STRICKEN...

WEAK... CAN'T MOVE! THIS MUST BE WHAT *IONA* MEANT WHEN SHE SAID THAT *ALDEBARAN* HAD EXTRAORDINARY POWERS! HE--HE'S USED THEM ON *ME*, I'M SURE OF IT! BUT I *CAN'T* LET HIM WIN THIS *DUEL* BETWEEN US!

THEN, IN HIS DILEMMA, A STARTLING IDEA SPRINGS INTO THE BRAIN OF THE *EMERALD CRUSADER*...

MAYBE... IT'S JUST POSSIBLE... THAT IF *I* CAN'T GO ON AND SEIZE *ALDEBARAN*-- MY *STATUE* CAN!! IT'S CLOSE ENOUGH TO ME... AND I STILL HAVE ENOUGH STRENGTH TO USE MY *POWER RING*! GOT TO TRY IT...!

THE NEXT MOMENT...

MY *POWER BEAM* HAS TURNED MY STATUE INTO A *SUPER-AUTOMATON*-- UNDER MY CONTROL! NOW I STILL HAVE A CHANCE TO DEFEAT THE MAGICIAN!

SNAP!

To GREEN LANTERN ERECTED IN ETERNAL GRATITUDE BY THE CITIZENS OF

SOON, THE METALLIC AVENGER--COUNTERPART OF THE GLADIATOR CONTROLLING IT--IS ON ITS WAY...

I'VE EQUIPPED THE *GREEN LANTERN* STATUE WITH AN INTERNAL MINIATURE TELEVISION CAMERA... AND THE MEANS OF PROJECTING WHAT IT "SEES" BACK TO ME HERE VIA MY BEAM! THIS WAY I CAN DIRECT ITS EVERY MOTION-- AS IT HEADS FOR ALDEBARAN!

15

AND SHORTLY, A HALF TON OF ADAMANT METAL CRASHES INTO ALDEBARAN'S HOUSE WITH THE FORCE OF A ROCKET BLAST...

BY THE SIGNS OF THE ZODIAC! MENTO-RAY--IT CAN HAVE NO EFFECT ON THIS STATUE OF HIMSELF THAT GREEN LANTERN HAS SENT AT ME!*

*Editor's Note: SINCE THE STATUE HAS NO BRAIN, THE MENTO-RAY WHICH IS DESIGNED TO ACT ON THE BRAIN, CANNOT HARM IT!

THEN, BEFORE ALDEBARAN CAN MAKE A MOVE TO FLEE...

UHH--

IN DESPERATION, THE BE-LEAGUERED MAGICIAN TRIES A MORE CONVENTIONAL WEAPON...

NOT EVEN A MISSILE-PISTOL CAN STOP IT!

GOT HIM! MY STATUE HAS KNOCKED ALDEBARAN OUT!

UHH--

NOW THAT I'VE CAPTURED THE MASTERMIND BEHIND THE REVOLT, I'LL GET HIM TO REVEAL THE REASON BEHIND IT!

16

IN DUE COURSE, UNDER GREEN LANTERN'S TRUTH BEAM, ALDEBARAN MAKES A COMPLETE CONFESSION...

...AND TWO YEARS AGO WHEN THE POST OF *SOLAR DIRECTOR* WAS VACANT I, WITH MY EXTRAORDINARY ABILITIES, SHOULD HAVE BEEN OFFERED IT-- INSTEAD OF *GREEN LANTERN!* SINCE THEN...

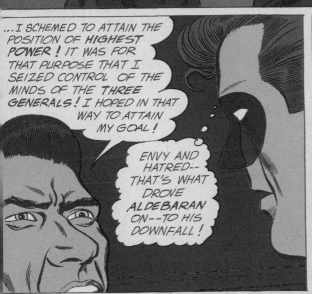

...I SCHEMED TO ATTAIN THE POSITION OF *HIGHEST POWER!* IT WAS FOR THAT PURPOSE THAT I SEIZED CONTROL OF THE MINDS OF THE *THREE GENERALS!* I HOPED IN THAT WAY TO ATTAIN MY GOAL!

ENVY AND HATRED-- THAT'S WHAT DROVE *ALDEBARAN* ON--TO HIS DOWNFALL!

LATER, WITH THE REVOLT OVER AND PEACE ONCE MORE REIGNING IN *STAR CITY*...

IONA, WE'VE HARDLY HAD A CHANCE TO SPEAK TO EACH OTHER! PERHAPS THIS EVENING--?

THERE'S NOTHING I WANT MORE IN THE WORLD!

BUT GREEN LANTERN DOESN'T REALIZE! NOW THAT HE'S SAVED US--AND PUT DOWN THE REBELLION-- HE MUST BE RETURNED *AT ONCE* TO HIS OWN ERA! AS CHAIRMAN DASOR HAS POINTED OUT, HIS *POWER RING* WOULD FAIL IF WE KEPT HIM HERE ANY LONGER--!

THE NEXT MOMENT...

HE'S-- HE'S GONE!

I KNOW HOW YOU MUST FEEL, *IONA*-- YOU MUST BE BRAVE, MY DEAR!

CHUCK!

THUS IT HAPPENS THAT BACK IN THE *GREEN GLADIATOR'S* DRESSING ROOM AT A CERTAIN MOMENT IN THE TWENTIETH CENTURY...

WHERE DID THIS TINY PIECE OF METAL COME FROM IN MY HAIR--?

Editor's Note: BY THE LAWS OF *TIME TRAVEL,* GREEN LANTERN HAS BEEN RETURNED TO HIS OWN ERA AT THE *EXACT MOMENT* HE LEFT IT, WITH NO LAPSE IN TIME!

17

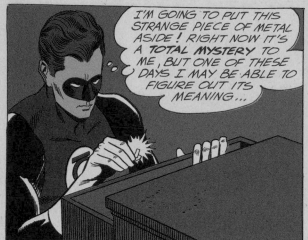

I'M GOING TO PUT THIS STRANGE PIECE OF METAL ASIDE! RIGHT NOW IT'S A *TOTAL MYSTERY* TO ME, BUT ONE OF THESE DAYS I MAY BE-ABLE TO FIGURE OUT ITS MEANING...

...AND WHY THE MERE SIGHT OF IT SHOULD AROUSE SUCH ODD, HIDDEN EMOTIONS DEEP WITHIN ME!

IN FAR-REMOVED STAR SQUARE IN THE DISTANT FUTURE, THE STATUE OF THE *EMERALD GLADIATOR* IS ONCE MORE ON ITS PEDESTAL WHERE *GREEN LANTERN'S* RING PLACED IT AFTER THE STATUE HAD RENDERED VALOROUS SERVICE...

AND THE STATUE LOOKS LIKE IT ALWAYS DID, A NOBLE REPRE-SENTATION OF THE JUSTICE — LOVING CRUSADER IN A MOMENT OF ACTION! BUT THERE IS A SMALL DIFFERENCE...

AT THE BASE OF THE STATUE NEAR ONE FOOT IS A LITTLE *SHINY SPOT!* IT SEEMS IN-SIGNIFICANT, BUT A VERY KEEN OBSERVER MIGHT DEDUCE THE TRUTH...

The End

...THAT A TINY PIECE OF THE METAL IS *MISSING,* AND WAS BROKEN OFF ON THE DAY WHEN *GREEN LANTERN'S STATUE WENT TO WAR!* 18

GREEN LANTERN

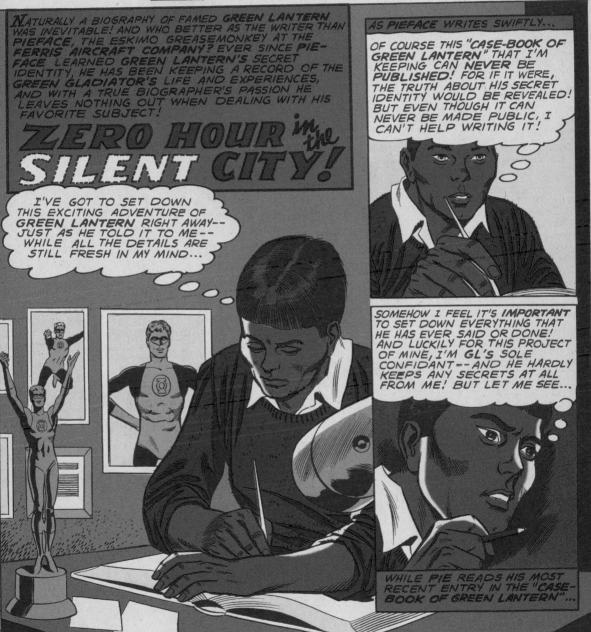

NATURALLY A BIOGRAPHY OF FAMED GREEN LANTERN WAS INEVITABLE! AND WHO BETTER AS THE WRITER THAN PIEFACE, THE ESKIMO GREASEMONKEY AT THE FERRIS AIRCRAFT COMPANY? EVER SINCE PIE-FACE LEARNED GREEN LANTERN'S SECRET IDENTITY, HE HAS BEEN KEEPING A RECORD OF THE GREEN GLADIATOR'S LIFE AND EXPERIENCES, AND WITH A TRUE BIOGRAPHER'S PASSION HE LEAVES NOTHING OUT WHEN DEALING WITH HIS FAVORITE SUBJECT!

ZERO HOUR in the SILENT CITY!

I'VE GOT TO SET DOWN THIS EXCITING ADVENTURE OF GREEN LANTERN RIGHT AWAY-- JUST AS HE TOLD IT TO ME-- WHILE ALL THE DETAILS ARE STILL FRESH IN MY MIND...

AS PIEFACE WRITES SWIFTLY...

OF COURSE THIS "CASE-BOOK OF GREEN LANTERN" THAT I'M KEEPING CAN NEVER BE PUBLISHED! FOR IF IT WERE, THE TRUTH ABOUT HIS SECRET IDENTITY WOULD BE REVEALED! BUT EVEN THOUGH IT CAN NEVER BE MADE PUBLIC, I CAN'T HELP WRITING IT!

SOMEHOW I FEEL IT'S IMPORTANT TO SET DOWN EVERYTHING THAT HE HAS EVER SAID OR DONE! AND LUCKILY FOR THIS PROJECT OF MINE, I'M GL'S SOLE CONFIDANT-- AND HE HARDLY KEEPS ANY SECRETS AT ALL FROM ME! BUT LET ME SEE...

WHILE PIE READS HIS MOST RECENT ENTRY IN THE "CASE-BOOK OF GREEN LANTERN"...

...LET US PEEK OVER HIS SHOULDER AND SEE WHAT HE HAS WRITTEN...

...and all that day test pilot Hal Jordan--alias Green Lantern--was completely absorbed in the activities of his daily life! All morning long he had been racking his brains over a technical problem involving stress on the wing of a new plane. Finally he rose, scratching his head wearily, wondering

PIE, I THINK IF I GET MY MIND AWAY FROM THIS PROBLEM AWHILE, IT MAY HELP ME SOLVE IT! I'M TAKING OFF-- TO RELAX!

CHECK, HAL! SOUNDS LIKE A GOOD IDEA--

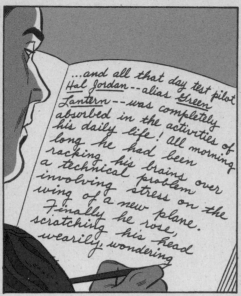

"THAT AFTER-NOON HAL RELAXED ALL RIGHT, ALONG WITH THOUSANDS OF OTHERS, AT THE BALL GAME!"

COME ON, RAMIS! BELT IT!

ONE MORE HOMER AND HE BREAKS THE RECORD!

"AFTER THE GAME..."

TERRIFIC!

GOSH, BASEBALL IS AN EXCITING SPORT! WHILE YOU'RE AT IT, YOU FORGET EVERYTHING ELSE! BUT I BETTER NOT FORGET THAT I'VE GOT A DATE WITH CAROL TONIGHT!

"SIX O'CLOCK FOUND HAL WITH HIS DATE--HIS YOUNG AND PRETTY BOSS CAROL FERRIS..."

...AND THEN I SAW RAMIS BELT ONE OVER THE FENCE!

MMM-- HOW THRILLING!

HOLDING CAROL THIS WAY IN MY ARMS IS ANOTHER THRILL-- BUT I WISH I COULD MANAGE IT WITHOUT USING DANCING AS AN EXCUSE!

"SUDDENLY, AS SOMETIMES HAPPENS, THE ELUSIVE ANSWER TO HIS PROBLEM OF THE MORNING POPPED INTO HAL'S HEAD!"

HAL, WHAT'S THE MATTER? YOU LOOK LIKE YOU'VE SEEN A GHOST!

I'VE GOT IT! I'VE GOT IT!

WHAT?! YOU'RE TAKING ME HOME?

I'M SORRY, CAROL! I'VE GOT TO GET BACK TO THE PLANT THIS EVENING! YOU SEE --

"ON THE WAY TO CAROL'S HOUSE, HAL EXPLAINED HIS 'WING STRESS' PROBLEM AND HIS EXCITEMENT IN SOLVING IT..."

... AND NOW I JUST CAN'T WAIT TO GET BACK TO MY DESK -- TO CHECK THE SOLUTION I'VE ARRIVED AT! AND ANYWAY, CAROL -- YOU DID SAY YOU WANTED TO GET HOME EARLY TONIGHT!

HMMM!

AS HAL'S EMPLOYER I CAN'T HELP BUT APPROVE HIS KEEN DEVOTION TO HIS JOB! BUT AS A GIRL I FEEL SOMETHING ELSE ENTIRELY! HE DIDN'T HAVE TO BRING ME HOME SO EARLY -- NO MATTER WHAT I SAID!

"HAL DROVE BACK THROUGH COAST CITY! IT WAS STILL DAYLIGHT AT THIS TIME OF YEAR..."

COME ON LIGHT, CHANGE!

≥YAWN≤ THIS HAS BEEN SOME DAY! THE BEAUTIFUL WEATHER... THE BALL GAME... DANCING WITH CAROL... AND SOLVING MY PROBLEM...!

"THEN..." IT'S A DAY LIKE THIS THAT MAKES LIFE-- EH? GREAT GUARDIANS! I'VE BEEN SO BUSY IT NEVER OCCURRED TO ME ONCE TODAY THAT MY POWER CHARGE ON MY RING WOULD RUN OUT ABOUT THIS TIME!

RATTATTA

EDITOR'S NOTE: WHEN THE POWER RING IS CHARGED IT RETAINS ITS POWER FOR EXACTLY TWENTY-FOUR HOURS!

TOOT! TOOT! EXTRA!

HONK!

BEEP!

I'VE ONLY GOT A FEW MINUTES OF POWER LEFT! IF I HAD TO CHANGE TO GREEN LANTERN NOW AND GO INTO ACTION-- I COULD EASILY WIND UP IN A FIX!...WILL THAT LIGHT NEVER CHANGE?

"THE NEXT MOMENT, AMAZINGLY..."

EH? THAT'S ODD...SUDDENLY THERE'S ABSOLUTE SILENCE ALL AROUND ME! THE CAR RADIO WAS BLASTING OUT-- NOW I CAN'T HEAR IT! I CAN'T HEAR ANYTHING!!

"AT FIRST HAL THOUGHT HIS HEARING MIGHT BE AFFECTED! BUT THEN HE REALIZED IT COULDN'T BE THAT..."

WHATEVER HAS HAPPENED-- EVERYONE IS AWARE OF IT! IT SEEMS TO BE CREATING CONFUSION-- AND NO WONDER! THIS INTERSECTION WAS LIKE A BOILER FACTORY A SECOND AGO...

...EVEN THAT SCREAMING WOMAN IS MAKING NO NOISE! PEOPLE HAVE LEFT THEIR CARS-- TRAFFIC IS STALLED!

SOMETHING TELLS ME THAT GREEN LANTERN BETTER DO SOME INVESTIGATING AT ONCE!

"IN THE COVER OF TREES IN A SMALL PARK NEARBY HAL SWIFTLY CHANGED TO THE UNIFORM OF HIS FAMED ALTER EGO..."

EVEN THOUGH THERE ARE ONLY A FEW MINUTES OF POWER LEFT IN MY RING, IT MAY BE ENOUGH TO GET TO THE BOTTOM OF THIS INCREDIBLE OCCURRENCE!

4

As the MYSTIC GREEN BEAM FANNED OUT EXPLORINGLY..."

CAUGHT SOMETHING! MY RING IS REVEALING...STRANGE **HIGH-FREQUENCY VIBRATIONS** COMING OUT OF THE THIRD FLOOR WINDOW OF THAT BUILDING OPPOSITE --

"UNHESITATINGLY, THE *GREEN GLADIATOR* ZOOMED UPWARD..."

BY MY RECKONING I HAVE EXACTLY **THIRTY SECONDS** OF RING-POWER LEFT! NO TIME TO GO BACK TO MY **POWER BATTERY** AND CHARGE IT! I'VE **GOT** TO TAKE THE RISK THAT IT WON'T **RUN OUT** ON ME!

"THEN..."

THIS ULTRA-HIGH SPEED **SUPERSONIC DRILL** IS SLICING INTO THE STEEL LIKE BUTTER! WE'LL HAVE THE SAFE OPEN IN TWO SHAKES --

TWENTY SECONDS OF POWER LEFT! GOT TO USE IT TO CORRAL THESE SAFE CRACKERS -- WITHOUT DELAY!

"BUT THE NEXT MOMENT..."

FRANKIE -- **LOOK!!**

THAT'S FUNNY -- I'M SHOUTIN' -- BUT CAN'T HEAR MY OWN VOICE!

A GOOD THING WE LEFT DANNY ON LOOKOUT!

HEY, NOW I CAN HEAR MYSELF!

GREEN LANTERN!? BOY, I SURE FLATTENED THAT BIG SHOT IN A HURRY!

5

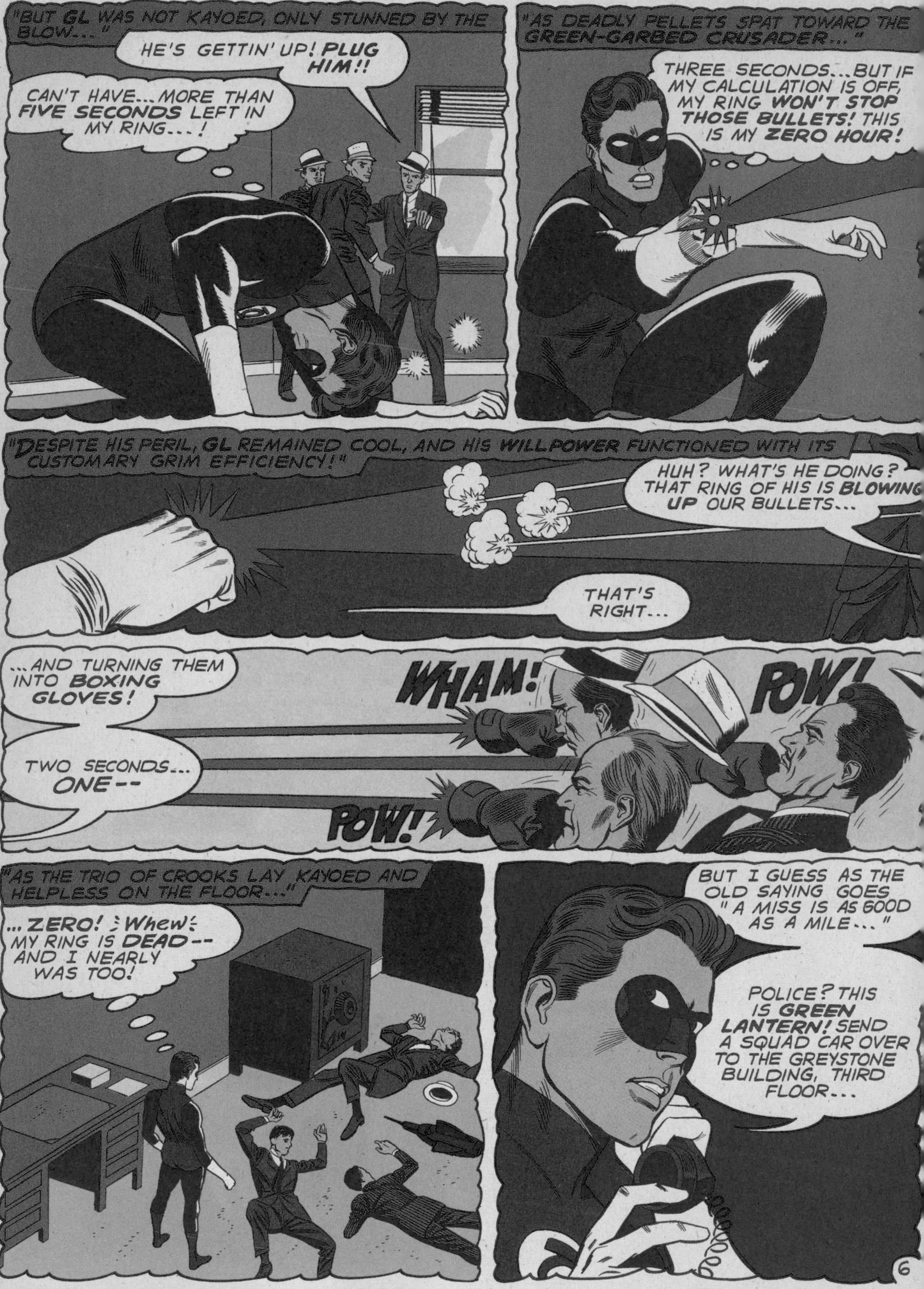
"BUT GL WAS NOT KAYOED, ONLY STUNNED BY THE BLOW..."
HE'S GETTIN' UP! PLUG HIM!!
CAN'T HAVE...MORE THAN FIVE SECONDS LEFT IN MY RING...!
"AS DEADLY PELLETS SPAT TOWARD THE GREEN-GARBED CRUSADER..."
THREE SECONDS...BUT IF MY CALCULATION IS OFF, MY RING WON'T STOP THOSE BULLETS! THIS IS MY ZERO HOUR!
"DESPITE HIS PERIL, GL REMAINED COOL, AND HIS WILLPOWER FUNCTIONED WITH ITS CUSTOMARY GRIM EFFICIENCY!"
HUH? WHAT'S HE DOING? THAT RING OF HIS IS BLOWING UP OUR BULLETS...
THAT'S RIGHT...
...AND TURNING THEM INTO BOXING GLOVES!
TWO SECONDS... ONE--
WHAM!
POW!
POW!
"AS THE TRIO OF CROOKS LAY KAYOED AND HELPLESS ON THE FLOOR..."
...ZERO! Whew MY RING IS DEAD-- AND I NEARLY WAS TOO!
BUT I GUESS AS THE OLD SAYING GOES "A MISS IS AS GOOD AS A MILE..."
POLICE? THIS IS GREEN LANTERN! SEND A SQUAD CAR OVER TO THE GREYSTONE BUILDING, THIRD FLOOR...
6

LATER, WITH THE CROOKS BEHIND BARS...

NO DOUBT IT WAS THIS AMAZING **SUPERSONIC** DRILL WHICH THOSE SAFECRACKERS DEVELOPED THAT CAUSED THE BLANKETING OF SOUND IN THIS PART OF THE CITY! AS SOON AS IT WAS STOPPED, SOUND CAME BACK!

YES! THE HIGH-SPEED VIBRATIONS FROM IT...

...SPREAD IN ABOUT A MILE-WIDE RADIUS AND SIMPLY CANCELED OUT **ORDINARY SOUND VIBRATIONS!** MY RING REVEALED THAT TO ME...

...BEFORE IT WENT DEAD!

"IN DUE COURSE, SHORTLY, A BELATED TASK WAS ATTENDED TO..."

IN BRIGHTEST DAY, IN BLACKEST NIGHT, NO EVIL SHALL ESCAPE MY SIGHT! LET THOSE WHO WORSHIP EVIL'S MIGHT BEWARE MY POWER--**GREEN LANTERN'S** LIGHT!

AT LAST! MY RING'S CHARGED FOR ANOTHER TWENTY-FOUR HOURS!

"**AND** THUS ENDED THIS **ZERO-HOUR** ADVENTURE OF **GREEN LANTERN!**"

AS GREEN LANTERN'S **UNOFFICIAL** BIOGRAPHER I INTEND TO PAY PARTICULAR ATTENTION TO THESE **ZERO-HOUR ADVENTURES** OF HIS! SO WHEN FURTHER EPISODES LIKE IT OCCUR, I'LL SET THEM RIGHT DOWN IN MY "**CASE-BOOK OF GREEN LANTERN!**"

CASE-BOOK OF GREEN LANTERN

The END

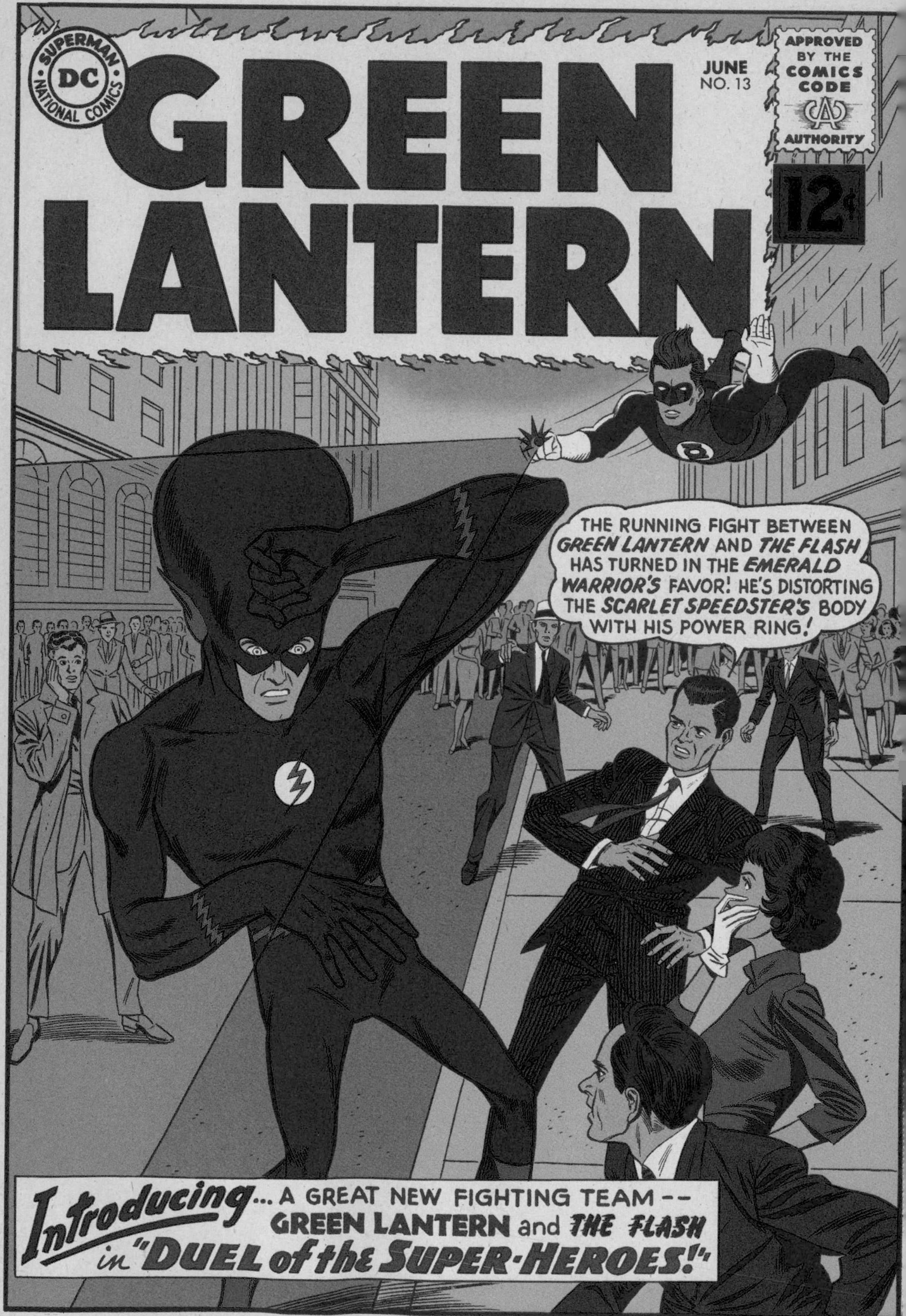

SUPERMAN DC NATIONAL COMICS
GREEN LANTERN
JUNE NO. 13
APPROVED BY THE COMICS CODE AUTHORITY
12¢
THE RUNNING FIGHT BETWEEN GREEN LANTERN AND THE FLASH HAS TURNED IN THE EMERALD WARRIOR'S FAVOR! HE'S DISTORTING THE SCARLET SPEEDSTER'S BODY WITH HIS POWER RING!
Introducing... A GREAT NEW FIGHTING TEAM -- GREEN LANTERN and THE FLASH in "DUEL of the SUPER-HEROES!"

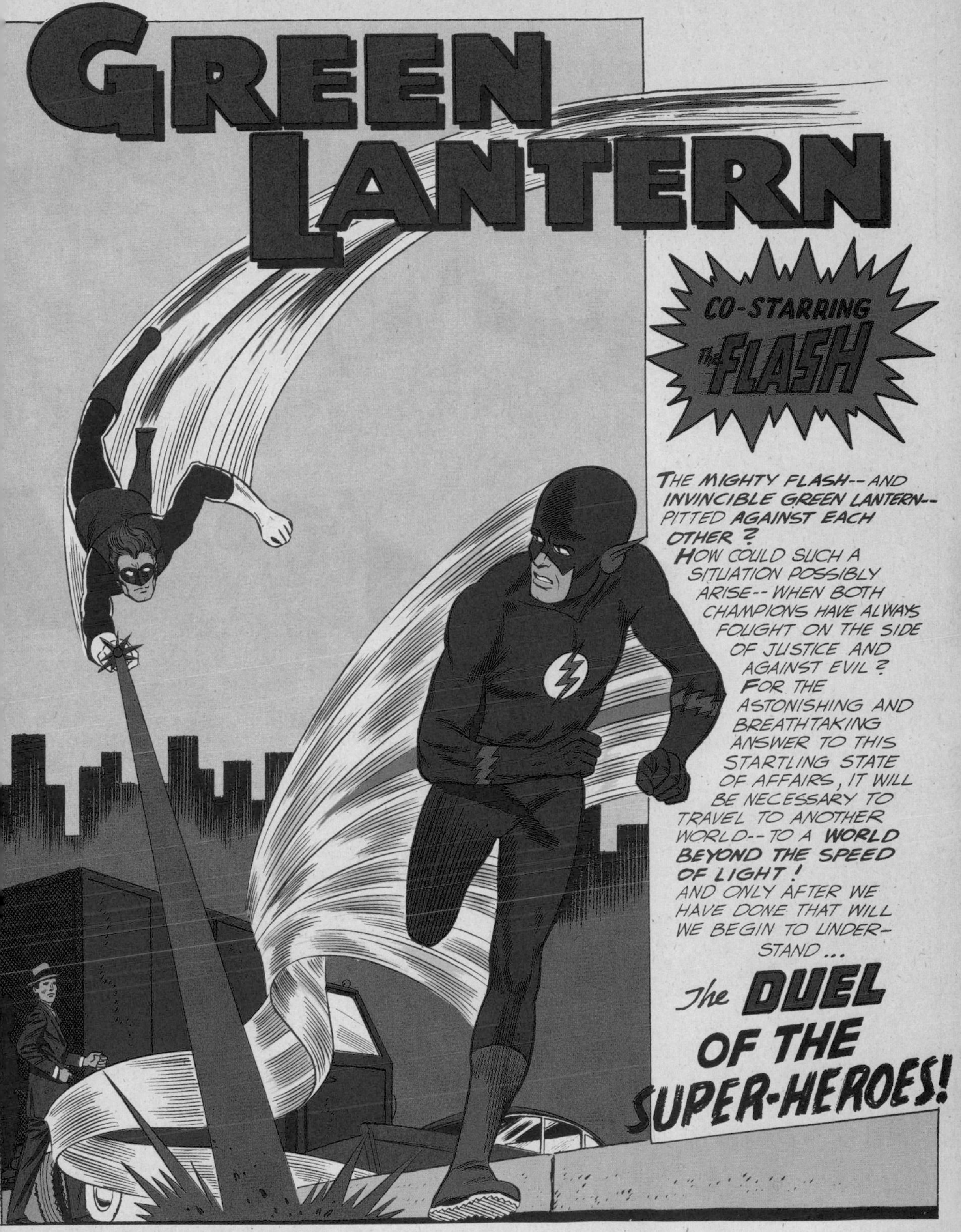
GREEN LANTERN
CO-STARRING The FLASH
THE MIGHTY FLASH--AND INVINCIBLE GREEN LANTERN--PITTED AGAINST EACH OTHER? HOW COULD SUCH A SITUATION POSSIBLY ARISE--WHEN BOTH CHAMPIONS HAVE ALWAYS FOUGHT ON THE SIDE OF JUSTICE AND AGAINST EVIL? FOR THE ASTONISHING AND BREATHTAKING ANSWER TO THIS STARTLING STATE OF AFFAIRS, IT WILL BE NECESSARY TO TRAVEL TO ANOTHER WORLD--TO A WORLD BEYOND THE SPEED OF LIGHT! AND ONLY AFTER WE HAVE DONE THAT WILL WE BEGIN TO UNDERSTAND...
The DUEL OF THE SUPER-HEROES!

IN THE **PICTURE NEWS** EDITORIAL OFFICE WHERE NEWSHEN IRIS WEST IS A STAR REPORTER...

"...AND MY BOY FRIEND **BARRY ALLEN** HAS AGREED TO TAKE HIS VACATION EARLY THIS YEAR AND ACCOMPANY ME TO THE WEST COAST! I HOPE IT'S ALL RIGHT WITH YOU, CHIEF...

SURE, IRIS! AS LONG AS YOU GET YOUR WORK DONE!

REMEMBER, YOU'LL HAVE TO INTERVIEW **HAL JORDAN**, THE FAMOUS TEST PILOT, ENOUGH TIMES TO DO THE **BIG STORY** ON HIM THAT WE WANT!

DON'T WORRY, CHIEF... YOU'LL GET YOUR STORY!

IN BARRY ALLEN'S APARTMENT, SHORTLY...

IRIS DOESN'T REALIZE IT BUT I HAVE **TWO** REASONS FOR GOING ALONG ON THIS TRIP! FIRST OF ALL I'D LIKE TO SPEND MY VACATION WITH HER, NATURALLY! BUT ALSO THERE'S SOMEONE I ADMIRE VERY MUCH OUT ON THE WEST COAST...

...NAMELY **GREEN LANTERN**! OF COURSE, IRIS DOESN'T SUSPECT THAT AS MY ALTER EGO, **THE FLASH**, I HAVE A SPECIAL FEELING FOR MY FELLOW **JUSTICE LEAGUE** MEMBER! AND I'M HOPING I HAVE THE LUCK TO MEET HIM WHILE I'M OUT THERE!

BUT I'D BETTER HURRY! THAT MUST BE IRIS NOW!

HONK! HONK!

BARRY-- SLOWPOKE! CAN'T YOU MOVE **FAST** FOR ONCE IN YOUR LIFE? WE'LL MISS THE PLANE!

COMING, IRIS! COMING!

TAXI

MEANWHILE, UNKNOWN TO BARRY (THE FLASH) ALLEN, HIS FELLOW-CRUSADER, GREEN LANTERN, HAS JUST WOUND UP A MISSION ON A FAROFF GALACTIC PLANET...

...AND IS RETURNING TO EARTH ALSO IN A BIT OF A HURRY!

THERE ARE A DOZEN MATTERS TO TAKE CARE OF AS SOON AS I GET HOME! GOT TO STEP ON IT-- REALLY TRAVEL!

AS ONE OF THE "MATTERS" IN PARTICULAR CLINGS IN THE MIND OF THE SPACE-CLEAVING GLADIATOR...

IN MY OTHER IDENTITY, AS HAL JORDAN, I'M DUE TO SPEND A HOLIDAY WEEK END AT THE SEASHORE WITH CAROL!* AND I WOULDN'T WANT TO MISS EVEN A MINUTE OF THAT!

*EDITOR'S NOTE: LOVELY CAROL FERRIS- HAL JORDAN'S BOSS AT THE FERRIS AIR-CRAFT COMPANY-- ALSO HAPPENS TO BE THE GIRL HE IS IN LOVE WITH!

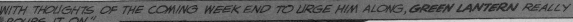

WITH THOUGHTS OF THE COMING WEEK END TO URGE HIM ALONG, GREEN LANTERN REALLY "POURS IT ON"...

THERE DOESN'T SEEM TO BE ANY LIMIT TO HOW FAST I CAN GO... BY BACKING MY RING WITH EVERY OUNCE OF MY WILL-POWER! AND THERE'S EARTH NOW!

THE NEXT INSTANT, INCREDIBLY...

BY THE GUARDIANS-- WHAT!?

THAT WALL--!!

TOO LATE, THE HURTLING GREEN-CLAD FIGURE BECOMES AWARE OF THE SOLID OBSTACLE BEFORE HIM...

SHOULD HAVE... KEPT MY RING GOING... TO PROTECT MYSELF! SUDDEN CHANGE... DAZED ME... UHHH!

3

WHEN THE STRICKEN RING-WIELDER COMES TO HIS SENSES...

WHERE AM I?

DO NOT FEAR! YOU ARE IN THE WORLD OF *SPECTAR*--OR AS YOU WOULD SAY IT...THE UNIVERSE BEYOND THE SPEED OF LIGHT! I AM *CHI-YAM*, THE CHIEF HERE! AND WE ARE ABLE TO SPEAK TO YOU...

...EVEN THOUGH WE DO NOT KNOW YOUR LANGUAGE, BECAUSE WE CAN COMMUNICATE DIRECTLY BY MEANS OF THOUGHT-PROJECTION!

BUT... HOW DID I GET HERE?

THAT IS SIMPLY TOLD! YOU HAPPENED TO BE TRAVELING *FASTER THAN LIGHT* AT THE *EXACT MOMENT* WHEN OUR TWO WORLDS--YOUR *EARTH* AND OUR *SPECTAR*-- COINCIDED IN HYPER-SPACE! BUT PERHAPS I HAD BETTER EXPLAIN...

"YOU SEE, IN HYPERSPACE THE ORBITS OF OUR TWO WORLDS ARE SOMEWHAT SIMILAR..."

"...WITH EACH IN ITS OWN DIMENSION, OF COURSE! BUT ONCE EVERY SPECTARN HIURN..."

"...WHICH EQUALS FOUR OF YOUR EARTH 'HOURS,' THE POSITIONS OF OUR TWO PLANETS *EXACTLY* COINCIDE!"

...AND AT THIS PRECISE MOMENT, TRAVEL BETWEEN OUR TWO WORLDS BECOMES AUTOMATIC BY ATTAINING A SPEED *GREATER THAN LIGHT!*

I SEE! STRANGE...

THESE PEOPLE SEEM SO *FRIENDLY* AND INTELLIGENT! YET... WHY IS IT I HAVE A *SINKING FEELING* INSIDE ME THAT... SOMETHING IS WRONG!?

WE KNOW HOW ANXIOUS YOU MUST BE TO RETURN TO YOUR *OWN WORLD!* THEREFORE, WE ARE READY TO HELP YOU DO SO, *GREEN LANTERN!*

eh? YOU KNOW MY NAME?!

I HAVEN'T THOUGHT MY NAME ONCE SINCE I CAME HERE--SO THEY DIDN'T LEARN IT BY READING MY MIND!

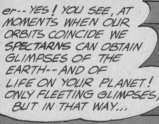

er--YES! YOU SEE, AT MOMENTS WHEN OUR ORBITS COINCIDE, WE SPECTARNS CAN OBTAIN GLIMPSES OF THE EARTH--AND OF LIFE ON YOUR PLANET! ONLY FLEETING GLIMPSES, BUT IN THAT WAY...

...WE LEARNED ABOUT YOU, *GREEN LANTERN*-- AND HOW YOU MUST CHARGE YOUR *POWER RING* EVERY TWENTY-FOUR HOURS! IT IS NOW NEARLY ONE *HILRN*-- FOUR HOURS--SINCE YOU CAME HERE! IF YOU STAY *TOO LONG* YOU WON'T HAVE ANY POWER TO RETURN...

THAT'S SO!

IT SEEMS THEY *DO* WANT TO HELP ME! I MUST GET OVER MY SILLY FEARS ABOUT THESE PEOPLE!

COME--THE MOMENT OF ORBIT-COINCIDING APPROACHES! YOU MUST NOT MISS IT!

5

IT MUST HAVE BEEN THE BLOW I... RECEIVED! MY HEAD ACHES SO...

NEVER MIND THAT! IT WILL GO AWAY... NOW YOU MUST HURRY...

...YOU MUST ATTAIN A SPEED FASTER THAN LIGHT QUICKLY-- TO TAKE YOU BACK TO YOUR OWN WORLD!

ALL RIGHT! FAREWELL...

AND SOON...

HE IS GONE!

HE ATTAINED THE PROPER SPEED-- AT THE PROPER MOMENT OF TIME *GREEN LANTERN* HAS GONE THROUGH TO HIS OWN DIMENSION!

YOU ARE--SURE WE DID RIGHT TO LET HIM GO, CHI-VAM?

OF COURSE, *GI-DOR!* WE COULD NOT REMOVE HIS INCREDIBLE RING--OR DUPLICATE IT! YOU SAW THAT! BESIDES...

...SHORTLY NOW WE SHALL HAVE HIS "FELLOW-GLADIATOR"-- THE EQUALLY-FAMOUS *FLASH*-- HELPLESS HERE IN OUR GRIP! AND ONCE WE LEARN FROM THIS *FLASH* THE SECRET OF *SUPER-SPEED*-- WHY, THE CONQUEST OF EARTH WILL BECOME SIMPLE!

6

DUEL OF THE SUPER-HEROES!

PART 2

SNAPPED BACK INTO HIS OWN UNIVERSE AT THE PRECISE MOMENT... AFTER HIS *POWER RING* HAD ENABLED HIM TO ATTAIN A SPEED GREATER THAN LIGHT... *GREEN LANTERN* FINDS HIS WAY SWIFTLY BACK TO EARTH AND THE MAIN HANGAR OF THE *FERRIS AIRCRAFT COMPANY*...

GREEN LANTERN! BOY, AM I GLAD TO SEE YOU! I WAS GETTING WORRIED! I KNEW IT WAS ALMOST TWENTY-FOUR HOURS SINCE YOU CHARGED YOUR RING--!

YES, THAT IS TRUE...

AS THOMAS (PIEFACE) KALMAKU, THE GREASE-MONKEY WHO IS GL'S SOLE CONFIDANT, WELCOMES HIS FAMED FRIEND.

I MUST RECHARGE MY RING RIGHT AWAY... TO BE PREPARED...

HUH?

IN HAL JORDAN'S DRESSING ROOM BEHIND A LOCKED DOOR...

WHAT'S WRONG WITH HIM? I'VE NEVER SEEN *GREEN LANTERN* ACT SO QUEER! HE MUST BE VERY *TIRED* OR SOMETHING--!

IN BRIGHTEST DAY, IN BLACKEST NIGHT...

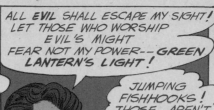

ALL *EVIL* SHALL ESCAPE MY SIGHT! LET THOSE WHO WORSHIP EVIL'S MIGHT FEAR NOT MY POWER-- *GREEN LANTERN'S LIGHT!*

JUMPING FISHHOOKS! THOSE...AREN'T THE WORDS TO HIS OATH!

WITH THE MYSTIC RING POWERED AGAIN FOR ANOTHER TWENTY-FOUR HOURS...

WHAT'S THE MATTER, *PIE-FACE?* WHY ARE YOU *STARING* AT ME LIKE THAT?

MAYBE I DIDN'T *HEAR RIGHT!* I-I WON'T SAY ANYTHING.

er-- YOU'D BETTER CHANGE TO YOUR HAL JORDAN OUTFIT, GL..

HAVE YOU FORGOTTEN WE'RE ALL GOING DOWN TO THE *SEA PALACE* THIS WEEK END? YOU AND CAROL AND TERGA AND I--!

SAY, THAT'S RIGHT. BE READY IN A MINUTE, *PIE!*

SHORTLY...

THE GIRLS ARE DOWN AT THE SEASHORE ALREADY, HAL! I TOLD THEM TO GO AHEAD AND THAT WE'D MEET THEM THERE! ALSO, WE'RE GOING TO HAVE ANOTHER COUPLE IN OUR PARTY THIS WEEK END...

ANOTHER COUPLE?

YES! *IRIS WEST*, A REPORTER FOR *PICTURE NEWS* HAS COME OUT HERE TO INTERVIEW YOU! HER ESCORT IS SOMEONE CALLED *BARRY ALLEN*, A POLICE SCIENTIST...

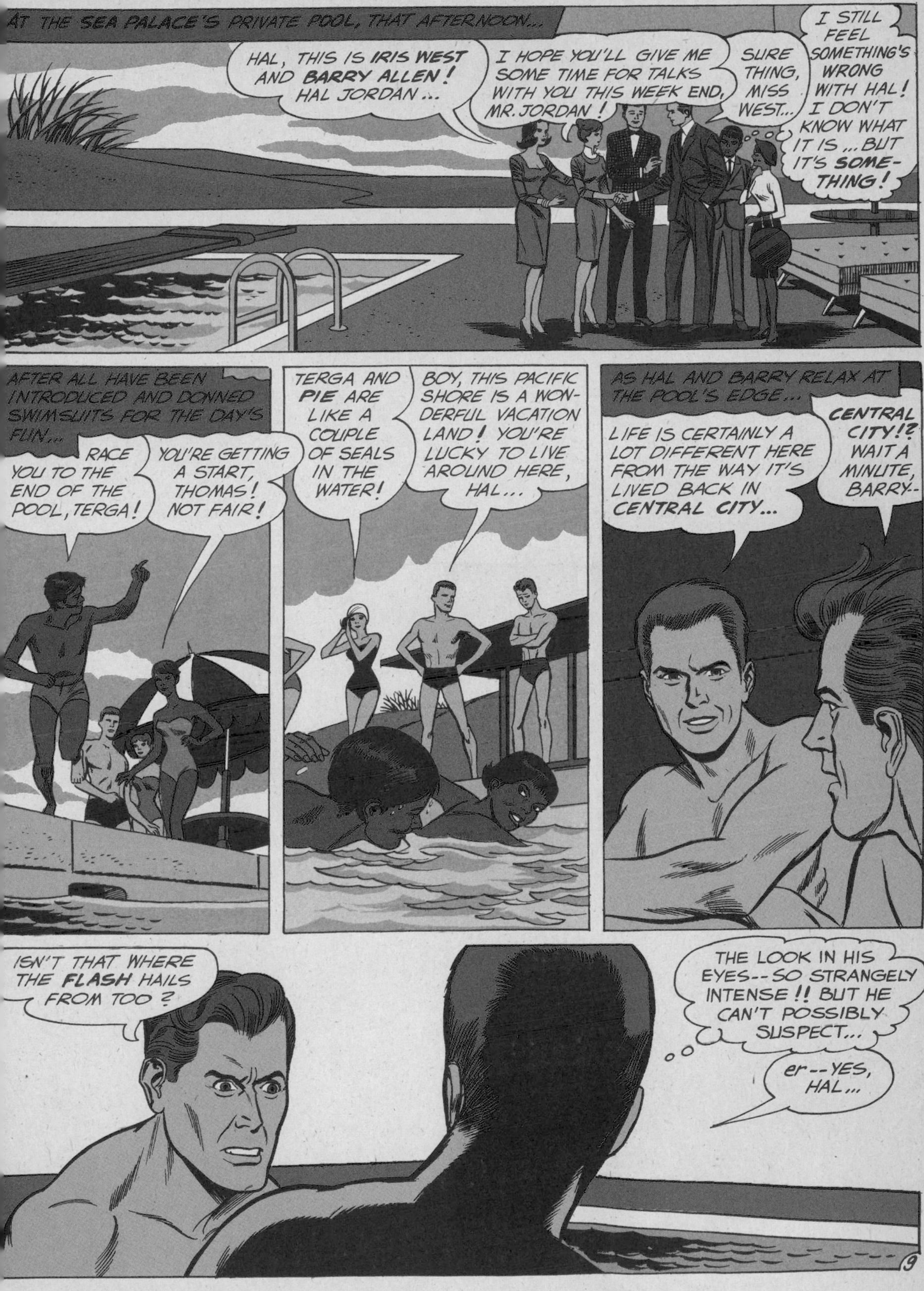
AT THE SEA PALACE'S PRIVATE POOL, THAT AFTERNOON...
HAL, THIS IS IRIS WEST AND BARRY ALLEN! HAL JORDAN...
I HOPE YOU'LL GIVE ME SOME TIME FOR TALKS WITH YOU THIS WEEK END, MR. JORDAN!
SURE THING, MISS WEST...
I STILL FEEL SOMETHING'S WRONG WITH HAL! I DON'T KNOW WHAT IT IS ... BUT IT'S SOMETHING!
AFTER ALL HAVE BEEN INTRODUCED AND DONNED SWIMSUITS FOR THE DAY'S FUN...
RACE YOU TO THE END OF THE POOL, TERGA!
YOU'RE GETTING A START, THOMAS! NOT FAIR!
TERGA AND PIE ARE LIKE A COUPLE OF SEALS IN THE WATER!
BOY, THIS PACIFIC SHORE IS A WONDERFUL VACATION LAND! YOU'RE LUCKY TO LIVE AROUND HERE, HAL...
AS HAL AND BARRY RELAX AT THE POOL'S EDGE...
LIFE IS CERTAINLY A LOT DIFFERENT HERE FROM THE WAY IT'S LIVED BACK IN CENTRAL CITY...
CENTRAL CITY!? WAIT A MINUTE, BARRY--
ISN'T THAT WHERE THE FLASH HAILS FROM TOO?
THE LOOK IN HIS EYES--SO STRANGELY INTENSE!! BUT HE CAN'T POSSIBLY SUSPECT...
er--YES, HAL...
9

WHAT MADE ME SAY THAT... ABOUT *THE FLASH?* IT... JUST POPPED OUT! AS IF... AS IF I HAVEN'T GOT CONTROL OF MY OWN TONGUE ANY MORE!

Hmm! I'M BEGINNING TO THINK THIS *HAL JORDAN* IS AN *ODD ONE!*

SHORTLY...

WHERE DID HAL GO?

HE WALKED DOWN THE BEACH-- SAID HE WANTED TO BE ALONE!

WELL, *THAT'S* SOCIABLE, I MUST SAY!

EXCUSE ME, TERGA, I WANT TO TALK... TO BARRY ALLEN...

GO AHEAD, THOMAS! WE GIRLS ARE GOING TO SUNBATHE NOW ANYHOW!

AS THE YOUNG ESKIMO LAD SEEKS OUT COUNSEL...

MR. ALLEN, YOU'RE A POLICE SCIENTIST! I'M WORRIED ABOUT MY PAL, HAL JORDAN... AND I THOUGHT I'D TELL YOU HE'S... JUST *NOT* ACTING *NORMAL!*

I CAN'T TELL HIM ABOUT THE OATH--THAT WOULD GIVE AWAY HAL'S SECRET IDENTITY AS *GREEN LANTERN!*

I NOTICED SOMETHING MYSELF, *PIE!* BUT-- WHAT DO YOU WANT ME TO DO?

I THOUGHT... IF THE TWO OF US KEPT AN EYE ON HIM... MAYBE WE'D FIGURE OUT WHAT WAS WRONG! PLEASE HELP ME, MR. ALLEN!

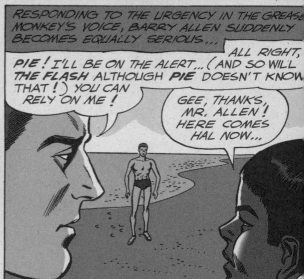

RESPONDING TO THE URGENCY IN THE GREASE MONKEY'S VOICE, BARRY ALLEN SUDDENLY BECOMES EQUALLY SERIOUS...

ALL RIGHT, *PIE!* I'LL BE ON THE ALERT... (AND SO WILL *THE FLASH* ALTHOUGH *PIE* DOESN'T KNOW THAT!) YOU CAN RELY ON ME!

GEE, THANKS, MR. ALLEN! HERE COMES HAL NOW...

NEXT DAY... I'VE NOTICED ONE THING, *PIEFACE!* EVERY FOUR HOURS HAL WANDERS OFF BY HIMSELF! HAS HE EVER DONE THAT SORT OF THING BEFORE?

NO, *NEVER!*

SEE--THERE HE GOES AGAIN! HE'S ALREADY EXCUSED HIMSELF TO THE GIRLS... TELL YOU WHAT, PIE--I'M GOING TO *FOLLOW HIM!*

I'LL GO WITH YOU!

NO, *PIE*--YOU STAY HERE! IT--er-- WILL BE BETTER THIS WAY!

ALL RIGHT-- IF YOU SAY SO! BUT-- GOLLY!

AS BARRY ALLEN SETS OUT AFTER HIS DIS-APPEARING QUARRY...

I DIDN'T WANT *PIEFACE* ALONG--BECAUSE I MAY HAVE TO CHANGE TO *THE FLASH* IN ORDER TO TRAIL HAL WITHOUT HIS SEEING ME! BUT HE DOESN'T SEEM TO SUSPECT SOMEONE MAY BE FOLLOWING HIM! HE HASN'T TURNED AROUND ONCE...

A QUARTER OF AN HOUR LATER... THE ROCKY HILLS ALONG HERE ARE LINED WITH CAVES--AND HE'S GOING INTO ONE OF THEM! WHAT IN THUNDER CAN HE BE UP TO--? I BETTER GO IN AFTER HIM...

IN THE DIMLY-LIT CAVERN... eh? HE'S TAKEN OFF HIS OUTER GARMENTS... THERE'S A *UNIFORM* ON UNDERNEATH... AND...

GREAT JUMPING JUPITER! IT'S *GREEN LANTERN'S* UNIFORM!

FROM CONCEALMENT BARRY WATCHES WIDE-EYED WITH FASCINATION AND CURIOSITY...

IT'S SOMETHING I NEVER DREAMED-- THAT HAL JORDAN IS REALLY GREEN LANTERN!

IT'S THE EXACT MOMENT OF ORBIT-COINCIDING...

...THE ONLY MOMENT EACH FOUR HOURS WHEN I CAN COMMUNICATE WITH MY MASTERS... THE SPECTARNS!

I HAVE NOT YET SEIZED THE FLASH FOR YOU! BUT I ASSURE YOU...

...I SHALL CARRY OUT MY MISSION! NOTHING WILL STOP ME!

WHAT'S WRONG WITH HIM? HE KEEPS STARING AT HIS POWER RING-- AS IF IN A TRANCE!

SUDDENLY, THE AROUSED POLICE SCIENTIST MAKES A DECISION...

I'VE GOT A FEELING THAT GREEN LANTERN IS IN TROUBLE! AND IF SO, HE-- MORE THAN ANYONE ELSE-- DESERVES TO HAVE THE FLASH AT HIS SIDE AT A TIME LIKE THIS!

SPURTING FROM A SECRET COMPARTMENT IN BARRY ALLEN'S RING, A FAMILIAR RED UNIFORM EXPANDS SWIFTLY-- BY A SPECIAL CHEMICAL FORMULA-- IN CONTACT WITH THE AIR...

AND A MOMENT LATER, WITH THE UNIFORM DONNED AT LIGHTNING BOLT VELOCITY BY THE FASTEST MAN ALIVE...

GREEN LANTERN, I WANT TO HELP YOU! IF YOU'LL TELL ME--

eh? THAT LOOK ON HIS FACE--IT'S FULL OF HATE-- FURY--!

...WITH GRIM INTENT, THE MYSTIC POWER BEAM FLARES OUT...

TRYING TO NET ME WITH THAT RING OF HIS!?

AS THE SCARLET SPEEDSTER TAKES EVASIVE ACTION--AT SUPER-SPEED...

HE MUST BE OUT OF HIS MIND! I WANT TO AID HIM AND HE ATTACKS ME! BUT I CAN'T STOP TO ARGUE--THAT POWER BEAM OF HIS IS TOO DANGEROUS!

INTO NEARBY COAST CITY THE WHIRLWIND CHASE EXTENDS...

CAN'T THROW HIM OFF MY TRAIL...

I'M TRAVELING AT LIGHT SPEED...

...BUT SO IS HE... RIGHT BEHIND ME...

THEN ON AN OPEN LOT IN THE CITY...

WHAT'S HE UP TO?

I GAINED A FRACTION OF A SECOND LEAD... AND MAYBE THAT'S ALL I NEED... TO USE MY SUPER-SPEED AND STIR UP THE EARTH HERE...

...INTO A WHIRLING, BLINDING DUST STORM! NOW... BEFORE GREEN LANTERN FINDS HIS WAY THROUGH THAT, I'LL BE FAR AWAY AND SAFE FROM HIS RING!

13

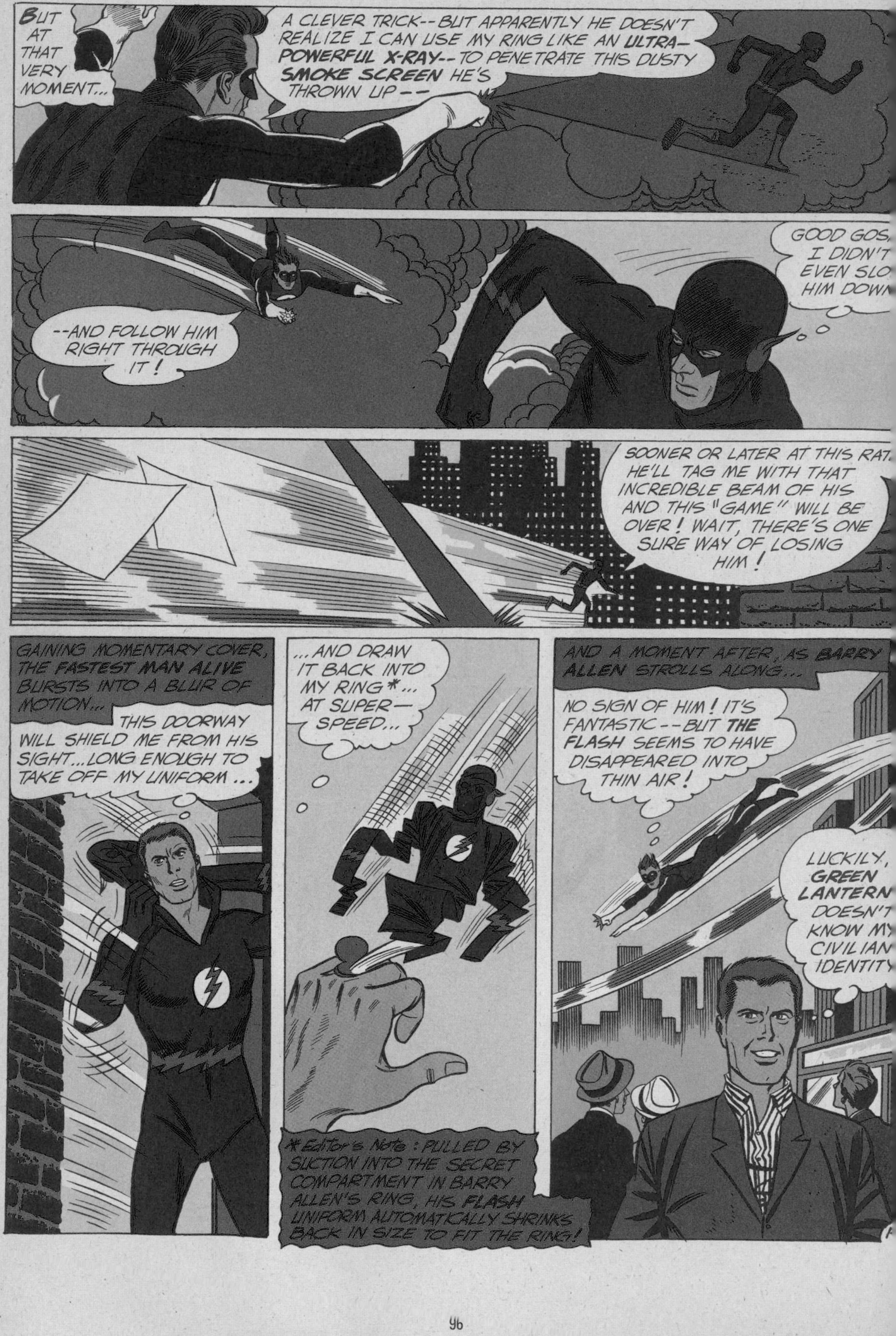

BUT AT THAT VERY MOMENT...
A CLEVER TRICK--BUT APPARENTLY HE DOESN'T REALIZE I CAN USE MY RING LIKE AN ULTRA-POWERFUL X-RAY--TO PENETRATE THIS DUSTY SMOKE SCREEN HE'S THROWN UP--
--AND FOLLOW HIM RIGHT THROUGH IT!
GOOD GOS, I DIDN'T EVEN SLO HIM DOWN
SOONER OR LATER AT THIS RAT HE'LL TAG ME WITH THAT INCREDIBLE BEAM OF HIS AND THIS "GAME" WILL BE OVER! WAIT, THERE'S ONE SURE WAY OF LOSING HIM!
GAINING MOMENTARY COVER, THE FASTEST MAN ALIVE BURSTS INTO A BLUR OF MOTION...
THIS DOORWAY WILL SHIELD ME FROM HIS SIGHT...LONG ENOUGH TO TAKE OFF MY UNIFORM...
...AND DRAW IT BACK INTO MY RING*...AT SUPER-SPEED...
*Editor's Note: PULLED BY SUCTION INTO THE SECRET COMPARTMENT IN BARRY ALLEN'S RING, HIS FLASH UNIFORM AUTOMATICALLY SHRINKS BACK IN SIZE TO FIT THE RING!
AND A MOMENT AFTER, AS BARRY ALLEN STROLLS ALONG...
NO SIGN OF HIM! IT'S FANTASTIC--BUT THE FLASH SEEMS TO HAVE DISAPPEARED INTO THIN AIR!
LUCKILY, GREEN LANTERN DOESN'T KNOW MY CIVILIAN IDENTITY

HE'S ESCAPED ME COMPLETELY! BUT I MUST FIND HIM! I MUST!

I'D BETTER RECHARGE MY RING...IT'S ALMOST TWENTY-FOUR HOURS SINCE I LAST CHARGED IT!

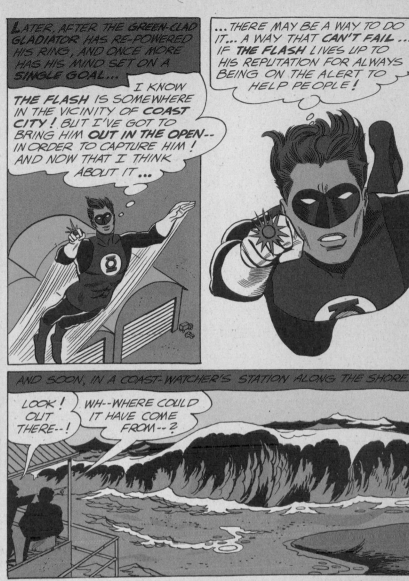

LATER, AFTER THE GREEN-CLAD GLADIATOR HAS RE-POWERED HIS RING, AND ONCE MORE HAS HIS MIND SET ON A SINGLE GOAL...

I KNOW THE FLASH IS SOMEWHERE IN THE VICINITY OF COAST CITY! BUT I'VE GOT TO BRING HIM OUT IN THE OPEN-- IN ORDER TO CAPTURE HIM! AND NOW THAT I THINK ABOUT IT...

...THERE MAY BE A WAY TO DO IT... A WAY THAT CAN'T FAIL... IF THE FLASH LIVES UP TO HIS REPUTATION FOR ALWAYS BEING ON THE ALERT TO HELP PEOPLE!

AND SOON, IN A COAST-WATCHER'S STATION ALONG THE SHORE...

LOOK! OUT THERE--!

WH--WHERE COULD IT HAVE COME FROM--?

INCREDIBLY, A MAMMOTH TIDAL WAVE HURTLES TOWARD THE BEACH AND COAST CITY...

SEND OUT AN ALARM! WARN THE PEOPLE! THAT WAVE COULD CAUSE UNTOLD DAMAGE--!

THEY DON'T REALIZE THE WAVE IS ONLY AN ILLUSION-- A MIRAGE--CREATED BY MY RING! IT CAN'T DO ANY HARM REALLY--BUT IF I'M RIGHT, IT WILL DRAW THE FLASH OUT INTO THE OPEN AGAIN!

15

SURE ENOUGH, IN THE CITY...

...TIDAL WAVE ABOUT TO SMASH THE CITY! RUN FOR HIGH GROUND! SAVE YOURSELVES--!

GREAT SCOTT! IN THIS EMERGENCY--

RADIO TV

...THE FLASH MUST HELP OUT-- TRY TO SAVE LIVES!

THE WAVE IS ALMOST ON US! ONLY A FEW MOMENTS LEFT...

AT THE SHORE, SPLIT-INSTANTS LATER, THE AMAZING SPEEDSTER SUCCEEDS, BY HIS INCOMPARABLE VELOCITY, IN ERECTING A GREAT DIKE OUT OF THE BEACH SAND TO BLUNT THE POWER OF THE ONCOMING GIANT ROLLER...

HERE COMES THE WAVE NOW! I HAVE ONLY A FEW SECONDS ...

...IN WHICH TO BUILD THIS SAND BARRIER...

...BUT A SECOND CAN BE A LONG TIME ...

...FOR ANYONE WHO CAN MOVE AS FAST AS I CAN!

MY BARRIER OUGHT TO STOP THAT MIGHTY WAVE...

...OR AT LEAST CUT DOWN ITS FORCE--!

16

THEN...

AHA! MY WAVE-MIRAGE FOOLED YOU TOO, **FLASH**, AND BROUGHT YOU OUT HERE TO STOP IT--JUST AS I FIGURED!

GREEN LANTERN AGAIN! BUT WHAT'S HE SAYING?

AS THE CRIMSON COMET BARELY AVOIDS THE ALL-POWERFUL BEAM OF HIS EMERALD-CLAD ADVERSARY...

THE TIDAL WAVE -- A MIRAGE? THEN ALL MY LABOR HAS BEEN FOR NOTHING! HE TRICKED ME BUT THERE'S STILL A CHANCE FOR ME TO ESCAPE HIS **TRAP**...

HE'S RIGHT BEHIND ME! I CAN ALMOST FEEL HIS BREATH ON MY NECK! BUT HE HASN'T GOT ME YET--

WHAT'S HE DOING? DOES **FLASH** IMAGINE HE CAN USE THAT BEACH UMBRELLA AS A WEAPON AGAINST MY RING--?

BUT AS GL DIVES IN FOR THE "KILL"...

UH? **GREAT GUARDIANS!** HE'S USING THE UMBRELLA AS A **SHIELD!** IT'S **YELLOW**-- AND MY RING CAN'T PENETRATE IT!

* Editor's Note: DUE TO A NECESSARY IMPURITY IN THE MATERIALS FROM WHICH IT WAS MADE, GREEN LANTERN'S POWER RING HAS NO EFFECT ON ANYTHING YELLOW!

17

LATER... A GOOD THING I REMEMBERED THAT GREEN LANTERN'S RING HAS NO EFFECT ON ANYTHING YELLOW! IT ENABLED ME TO ESCAPE HIM ONCE AGAIN! BUT ALSO--THE THOUGHT HAS OCCURRED TO ME--

--THAT IF I KEEP ELUDING THE EMERALD GLADIATOR I MAY NEVER LEARN WHAT'S WRONG WITH HIM--AND WHY HE IS TRYING TO CAPTURE ME! FOR GREEN LANTERN'S SAKE, I KNOW WHAT I MUST DO...

I MUST LET HIM CAPTURE ME! IT'S THE ONLY WAY I CAN THINK OF TO GET TO THE BOTTOM OF THIS MYSTERY! IT MEANS TAKING A DANGEROUS CHANCE--BUT I'VE GOT TO RISK IT!

SOON AFTER... THERE HE IS! THIS TIME I'LL MAKE SURE THE FLASH DOESN'T ESCAPE ME BY SOME SUPER-SPEED TRICK! I'M GOING TO FIX HIM SO HE CAN'T USE HIS FANTASTIC SPEED--!

WH-WHAT'S HAPPENING TO ME?

BY INCREASING THE SIZE OF THE UPPER PORTION OF HIS BODY, MY RING IS MAKING HIM SO TOP HEAVY HE WON'T BE ABLE TO MOVE FASTER THAN A TURTLE! I'VE GOT HIM NOW!

AND SURE ENOUGH...

IN A FEW MINUTES IT WILL BE ORBIT-COINCIDING TIME AGAIN--AND I WILL BE ABLE TO TURN OVER THE FLASH TO MY MASTERS, THE SPECTARNS--IN THE WORLD BEYOND THE SPEED OF LIGHT!

DUEL OF THE SUPER-HEROES PART 3

UNDER A HYPNOTIC SPELL CAST OVER HIM BY THE INCREDIBLE SPECTARNS, GREEN LANTERN HAS DUTIFULLY DELIVERED THE FLASH TO THEM IN THE UNIVERSE BEYOND THE SPEED OF LIGHT! AND NOW AS THE SCARLET SPEEDSTER--RETURNED TO NORMAL SIZE AGAIN BY GREEN LANTERN--LIES UNCONSCIOUS BUT HELPLESS UNDER IMPRISONING RADIATION, THE GREEN-GARBED CRUSADER--NO LONGER NEEDED--IS SENT BACK TO EARTH, AFTER STEPS HAVE BEEN TAKEN TO INSURE THAT HE CANNOT INTERFERE WITH THE CAREFULLY-LAID PLANS OF HIS "MASTERS"!

GREEN LANTERN'S RING PROTECTS HIM FROM MORTAL HARM... SO WE HAVE ORDERED HIM BACK TO HIS WORLD... BUT WITH ALL **MEMORY** OF US AND WHAT HAPPENED HERE WIPED COMPLETELY FROM HIS MIND!

WE HAVE ALREADY PROVED THAT WE CAN HANDLE **GREEN LANTERN**! HE WILL BE NO OBSTACLE TO US IN OUR FORTHCOMING **MILITARY ACTION**!

ACCORDING TO THEIR THOUGHTS REACHING ME, THESE **SPECTARNS** SEIZED CONTROL OF **GREEN LANTERN**--AND **THAT'S** WHY HE BROUGHT ME HERE-- FOLLOWING THEIR **MENTAL ORDERS**! BUT--

19

WHY DID THEY WANT *ME*?! WHAT DO THEY HOPE TO GAIN FROM HAVING *ME* A PRISONER?

IT'S VERY SIMPLE, *FLASH*...

AS THE SPECTARN LEADER SURPRISINGLY ANSWERS THE UNSPOKEN QUERY OF HIS CAPTIVE...

YOU SEE, THE ONLY WAY TO PASS BETWEEN OUR WORLD AND YOURS IS TO TRAVEL AT A **SPEED GREATER THAN LIGHT**! LONG HAVE OUR SPECTARN WARRIORS BEEN READY TO **INVADE AND CONQUER YOUR EARTH**! OUR ONLY PROBLEM HAS BEEN TO **GET THERE**!

THAT PROBLEM WE WILL NOW SOLVE -- BY ANALYZING WITH OUR ULTRA-SCIENTIFIC METHODS **YOUR SUPER-SPEED ABILITY**! ONCE WE HAVE THE ANSWER, WE WILL ENDOW ALL OUR WARRIORS WITH **SUPER-LIGHT SPEED** TO ENABLE THEM TO BREAK THROUGH THE DIMENSION BARRIER!

AND UNFORTUNATELY FOR YOU, MY DEAR "SPEEDSTER," THERE IS *NOTHING* YOU CAN DO TO STOP US!

START THE **COMPUTO-ANALYZER**...

THEN, TO FLASH'S ASTONISHMENT, THOUGHTS POUR FROM THE ACTIVATED MACHINE...

...THE SOURCE OF THE ...REMARKABLE SPEED OF THE ...LIFE-FORM BEFORE ME... IS A ...COMPLICATED **CHEMICAL ACCIDENT** WHICH ALTERED THE STRUCTURE OF HIS BODY! I WILL NOW LIST THE **CHEMICAL CHANGES** THAT TOOK PLACE AT THAT TIME ...

GREAT SCOTT! IT IS PROBING THE SECRET OF MY SUPER-SPEED...!

BUT MEANWHILE WHAT OF **GREEN LANTERN**? ODDLY ENOUGH THE **EMERALD GLADIATOR** HAS RETURNED TO EARTH, LABORING UNDER A PECULIAR ILLUSION!

WITH ALL MEMORY OF HIS ENCOUNTER WITH THE **SPECTARNS** ERASED FROM HIS MIND, HE IS UNDER THE IMPRESSION THAT IT IS THE **PREVIOUS DAY**, WHEN HE WAS RETURNING FROM HIS OUTER-SPACE MISSION!

FERRIS AIRCRAFT COMPANY

NO SIGN OF **PIEFACE**! Hmm! I'LL BET HE AND TERGA AND CAROL WENT DOWN TO THE **SEA PALACE** RESORT AND ARE WAITING FOR ME THERE!

SOON AFTER, HAL JORDAN IS DRIVING TOWARD THE SHORE...

I CALLED CAROL'S HOUSE BUT THERE WAS NO ANSWER! SO I GUESS I WAS RIGHT ABOUT HER GOING AHEAD WITH **PIE** AND TERGA! BUT I'LL HAVE TO INVENT SOME KIND OF EXCUSE TO EXPLAIN MY BEING LATE! CAROL HASN'T THE FAINTEST IDEA I'M REALLY **GREEN LANTERN**...

SURE ENOUGH THERE'S **PIEFACE**!

HI, PIE--!

HAL! WHERE HAVE YOU BEEN?! WE'VE BEEN WORRIED SICK ABOUT YOU--

--SINCE YOU DISAPPEARED THIS MORNING WITH BARRY ALLEN!

SINCE I **DISAPPEARED**... WITH BARRY ALLEN?! PIE, WAIT A MINUTE, HOLD EVERYTHING! WHO.. IS BARRY ALLEN!?

HAL--WHAT'S GOT INTO YOU? SURELY YOU REMEMBER BEING HERE THIS MORNING--YOU WENT OFF ALONG THE BEACH AND BARRY ALLEN FOLLOWED YOU!

I WAS... **HERE** THIS MORNING..!?

AS GRIM THOUGHTS GROUND INTO THE BRAIN OF THE CRACK TEST PILOT...

THIS FITS IN WITH A STRANGE FEELING I'VE HAD DURING THE LAST HOUR THAT I COULDN'T EXPLAIN... A FEELING THAT SOMETHING TERRIBLE WAS ABOUT TO HAPPEN! BUT WHAT? HOW COULD I HAVE BEEN HERE BEFORE... AND NOT KNOW IT?!

21

SUDDENLY... PIE, LISTEN--SAY NOTHING TO CAROL OR ANYONE ELSE HERE ABOUT MY ARRIVAL! I'VE GOT TO UN-RAVEL THIS MYSTERY--AND SOMETHING TELLS ME I'VE GOT TO DO IT FAST-- WITHOUT A MOMENT'S DELAY!

UH--OKAY, HAL!

I'LL TELL THE GIRLS THAT YOU AND... BARRY ALLEN... WENT OFF FISHING TODAY... ALL RIGHT?

RIGHT! SEE YOU LATER!

ALONG A BARREN STRETCH OF BEACH...

I'VE LOST A DAY OUT OF MY LIFE --SOME-HOW! BUT AS SURE AS I'M GREEN LANTERN, I'M GOING TO GET BACK THAT DAY!

RAISING HIS MYSTIC POWER RING, GREEN LANTERN GIVES IT A STERN MENTAL COMMAND...

RING, TELL ME EVERYTHING THAT HAPPENED TO ME DURING THE LAST TWENTY-FOUR HOURS -- AND LEAVE NOTHING OUT!

UNDER THE EMERALD WARRIOR'S DRIVING WILL-POWER, HIS AMAZING RING RESPONDS...

...YOU WERE FLYING THROUGH SPACE... GOING AT A TREMENDOUS RATE... IN ORDER TO REACH EARTH IN TIME FOR YOUR DATE...

"SUDDENLY, YOU EXCEEDED THE SPEED OF LIGHT AND AT THAT MOMENT AS YOU ENTERED THE WORLD OF SPECTAR..."

...I CRASHED AND KNOCKED MYSELF OUT! YES, IT'S COMING BACK TO ME NOW--

...AS THE MYSTIC RING CONCLUDES ITS DETAILED ACCOUNT OF THE MISSING TWENTY-FOUR HOURS...

...AND THEN YOU WERE SENT BACK TO EARTH WITH ALL MEMORY OF THE ENTIRE DAY WIPED FROM YOUR MIND!

IT'S CLEAR NOW! THE SPECTARNS ALMOST SUCCEEDED IN THEIR DIABOLIC SCHEME!

--BUT THEY SLIPPED UP BY NOT REALIZING THAT MY RING WOULD AUTOMATICALLY RECORD EVERYTHING THAT HAPPENED TO ME! AND NOW TO MAKE THEM PAY FOR THAT MISTAKE!

IN THE WORLD BEYOND THE SPEED OF LIGHT, SHORTLY AFTERWARD...

THE COMPUTO-ANALYZER HAS GIVEN US THE COMPLETE CHEMICAL PROCESS--THE SECRET OF SUPER-SPEED!

NOTHING NOW CAN PREVENT US FROM INVADING AND CONQUERING THE EARTH!

I'VE GOT TO GET LOOSE!

BUT I CAN'T EVEN VIBRATE! THAT RADIATION ON ME... HOLDING ME ABSOLUTELY RIGID--eh?

THEN...

MAYBE THIS WILL HELP YOU GET FREE, FLASH!

GREEN LANTERN-- USING HIS RING TO SMASH THE RAY-MACHINE BEAMED AT ME--!

BUT IN THE MOMENT THAT THE *EMERALD GLADIATOR* TAKES TO FREE HIS COSTUMED ALLY, THE DAZED *SPECTARNS* RECOVER AND STRIKE WITH SURPRISING SPEED...

TECTS **GREEN LANTERN** FROM DESTRUCTION--BUT OUR **NEUTRON GUNS** CAN STILL RENDER HIM UN-CONSCIOUS LONG ENOUGH FOR US TO MAKE HIM A PRISONER!

THEIR RAY-WEAPONS HAVE HIT **GREEN LANTERN**--HE'S FALLING--!

LIKE A *MADDENED TORNADO*, THE *WORLD'S FASTEST HUMAN* BURSTS INTO A FURY OF MOTION, ROUNDING THE ROOM SO SWIFTLY HE IS ALL BUT INVISIBLE AS HE DISARMS HIS FOES BEFORE THEY CAN DO ANY MORE DAMAGE...

GOT TO GIVE **GL** A CHANCE-- TO COME TO HIS SENSES! AND I...

¡Whew!¡ I FEEL NUMB...BUT I CAN'T LET THAT KEEP ME DOWN--!

...MUST MAKE SURE NO FURTHER SHOTS ARE AIMED AT HIM--BY KNOCKING ALL THESE WEAPONS....

...OUT OF THE HANDS OF THE *SPECTARNS!*

THE NEXT MOMENT, AS THE GREAT GREEN BEAM IS TURNED ONCE AGAIN TO THE ATTACK...

SPARE US! WAIT! DO NOT DESTROY US--!

BEGGING FOR THEIR LIVES--

WE MIGHT HAVE GUESSED, **FLASH!** WOULD-BE CONQUERORS ARE ALWAYS **COWARDS** AT HEART!

LATER, WITH THE RULING CLIQUE OF SPECTAR SAFELY BEHIND BARS, GREEN LANTERN AND FLASH MEET WITH ANOTHER, LESS WARLIKE SECTION OF THE POPULACE...

YOU DRONES HAVE ALWAYS BEEN THE WORKHORSES OF SPECTAR! WE ARE GOING TO GIVE YOU A CHANCE TO GOVERN HERE--PROVIDING YOU PUT ASIDE ALL THOUGHTS OF WAR AND DEVOTE YOURSELVES TO PURSUITS OF PEACE!

WE PROMISE, O EARTHLING! WE HAVE ALWAYS HATED WAR!

DO YOU THINK WE CAN TRUST THESE DRONES, GREEN LANTERN?

I THINK WE CAN, FLASH! MY RING HAS SHOWN ME THAT THEY ARE SINCERE IN THEIR PROMISES! BUT JUST TO MAKE SURE...

...I'LL USE MY BEAM TO DESTROY THIS PAPER PRODUCED BY THE COMPUTO-ANALYZER THAT REVEALED HOW YOUR SUPER-SPEED CAN BE DUPLICATED!

GOOD! AND I'LL TAKE ONE MORE PRECAUTION...

AS A FIERCE VACUUM CREATED BY THE FASTEST MAN ALIVE LITERALLY PULLS THE COMPUTO-ANALYZER TO PIECES...

LATER, BACK IN THEIR OWN FAMILIAR WORLD, TWO HEROES RELAX FOR THE FIRST TIME IN MANY HOURS...

...AND THAT'S HOW I LEARNED YOU WERE REALLY HAL JORDAN, GREEN LANTERN-- BY FOLLOWING YOU! BUT NOW I THINK IT'S ONLY FAIR TO REVEAL TO YOU WHAT MY SECRET IDENTITY IS!

WELL, I AM CURIOUS, FLASH--I'LL ADMIT IT!

NOW MY SECRET OF SUPER-SPEED IS SAFE AGAIN--AND EARTH IS SAFE FROM ANY POSSIBLE INVASION FROM SPECTAR!

THAT DOES IT, FLASH!

25

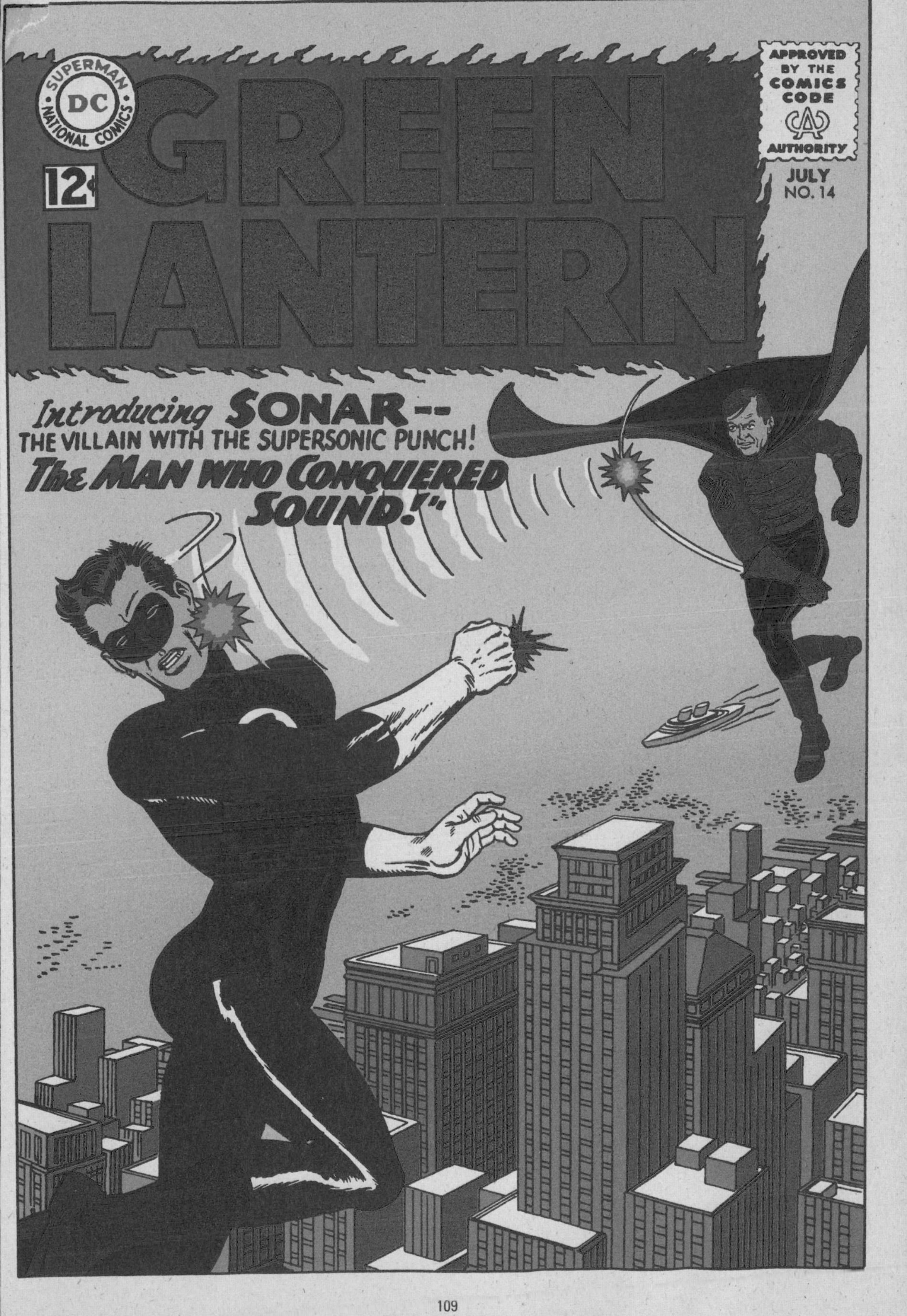
SUPERMAN
DC
NATIONAL COMICS
12¢
GREEN LANTERN
APPROVED BY THE COMICS CODE AUTHORITY
JULY
NO. 14
Introducing SONAR--
THE VILLAIN WITH THE SUPERSONIC PUNCH!
"The MAN WHO CONQUERED SOUND!"

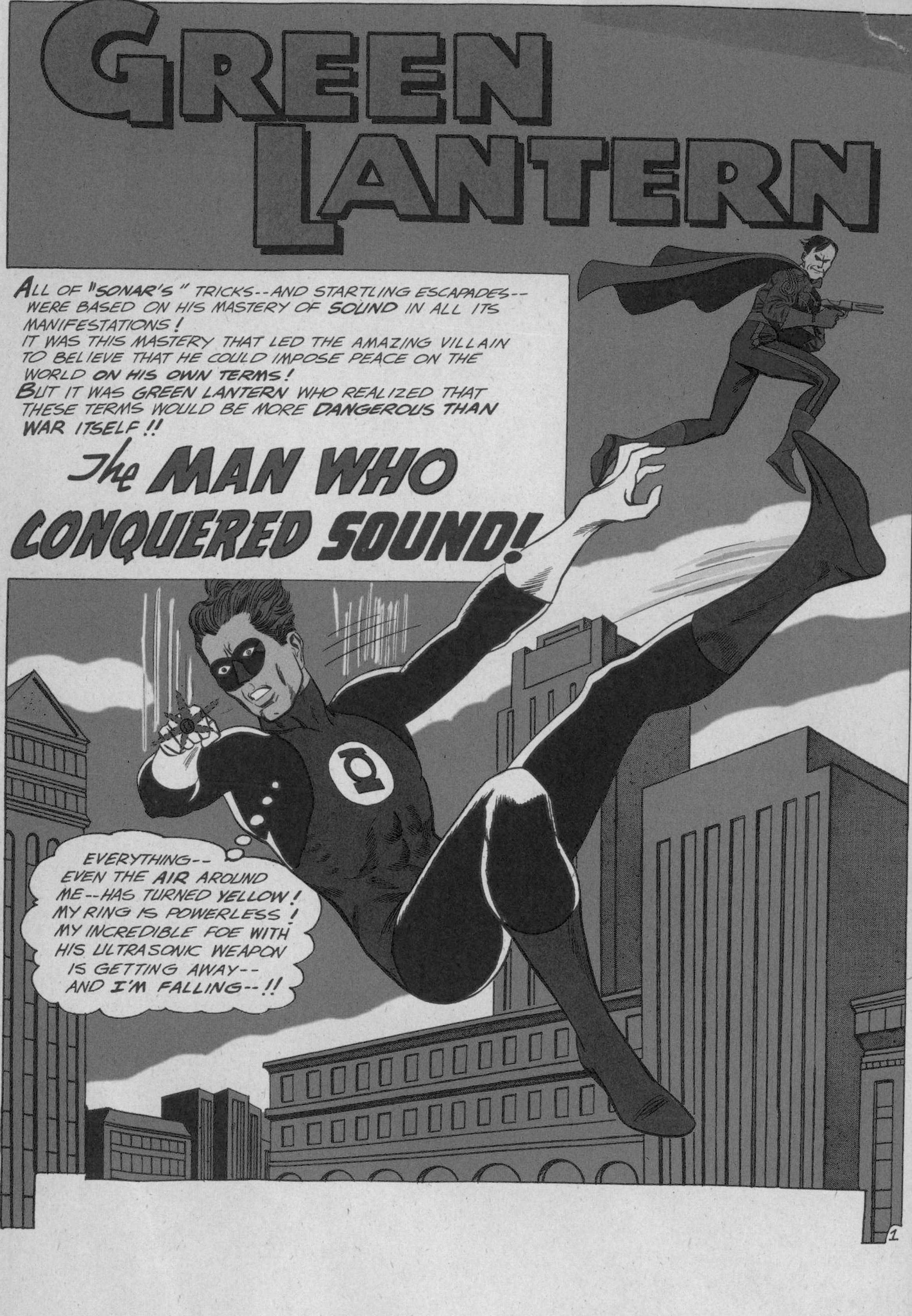
GREEN LANTERN
ALL OF "SONAR'S" TRICKS--AND STARTLING ESCAPADES--WERE BASED ON HIS MASTERY OF SOUND IN ALL ITS MANIFESTATIONS! IT WAS THIS MASTERY THAT LED THE AMAZING VILLAIN TO BELIEVE THAT HE COULD IMPOSE PEACE ON THE WORLD ON HIS OWN TERMS! BUT IT WAS GREEN LANTERN WHO REALIZED THAT THESE TERMS WOULD BE MORE DANGEROUS THAN WAR ITSELF!!
The MAN WHO CONQUERED SOUND!
EVERYTHING-- EVEN THE AIR AROUND ME--HAS TURNED YELLOW! MY RING IS POWERLESS! MY INCREDIBLE FOE WITH HIS ULTRASONIC WEAPON IS GETTING AWAY-- AND I'M FALLING--!!
1

RETURNING HOME FROM A COSMOS-WIDE MEETING OF HIS FELLOW GREEN LANTERNS, THE EMERALD GLADIATOR OF EARTH RECALLS SOMETHING...

THERE'S EUROPE BELOW ME... AND IT REMINDS ME! PIEFACE AND I WERE HAVING A CHAT THE OTHER DAY... HE'S AN AVID STAMP COLLECTOR...

"...AND HE WAS SHOWING ME HIS STAMP ALBUM.."

I'VE GOT STAMPS FROM EVERY COUNTRY IN THE WORLD, HAL-- EXCEPT ONE! IF I HAD A MODORA STAMP, MY COLLECTION WOULD BE COMPLETE!

MODORA? I DON'T BELIEVE I EVER HEARD OF IT!

VERY FEW PEOPLE HAVE! IT'S A TINY COUNTRY IN THE BALKANS!--SO SMALL IT'S NOT EVEN IN THE UNITED NATIONS! AND NO ONE I KNOW HAS A STAMP FROM THERE! BOY, IF I COULD ONLY GET ONE--!

PIE SURE HAS A LONGING FOR THAT STAMP...

I DECIDED THEN THAT IF I EVER HAD A CHANCE TO GET A--er--MODORA STAMP FOR PIEFACE*, I WOULD DO SO! AND NOW'S MY OPPORTUNITY-- ON MY WAY HOME!

*Editor's Note: THE HAPPY-FACED ESKIMO LAD WHO IS THE GREASEMONKEY OF TEST PILOT HAL JORDAN--ALIAS GREEN LANTERN!

SOON, AFTER A SHARP-EYED SEARCH...

THIS IS IT--MODORA... ALMOST SWALLOWED UP HERE IN THE MOUNTAINS OF SOUTH-EASTERN EUROPE...

BUT WHEN GREEN LANTERN POLITELY ADDRESSES ONE OF THE INHABITANTS...

GORIG GAMUDO IGORN?

GOOD GOSH! I FORGOT THEY DON'T SPEAK ENGLISH! BUT MY POWER RING CAN FIX THAT...

As the great green beam is put to use in a novel way, setting up automatic mental communication...

I CAN UNDERSTAND HER NOW! BUT--WHAT'S SHE SAYING--?

THAT COSTUME--HOW YOU FLY-- YOU MUST BE A CREATURE FROM--ANOTHER WORLD!

NO, MADAM! MY NAME IS GREEN LANTERN AND I'M FROM AMERICA! AND I'M--er--LOOKING FOR A STAMP...!

A STAMP? GOODNESS ME! I DON'T HAVE ONE...

WE NEVER MAIL LETTERS IN MOORA! WHY SHOULD WE? EVERYONE HERE LIVES WITHIN WALKING DISTANCE OF EVERYONE ELSE!

Hmmm! THIS IS ANNOYING...

I'LL TRY SOMEONE ELSE! THERE'S BOUND TO BE A STAMP HERE! AND NO MATTER HOW SMALL THIS PLACE IS, IT'S GOT TO HAVE A POST OFFICE! BUT I CAN'T WASTE A LOT OF TIME--I KNOW WHAT I'LL DO...

I'LL SIMPLY USE MY RING TO PROBE THE MIND OF THE FIRST LIKELY-- LOOKING IN-DIVIDUAL I SEE! THAT WAY I'LL FIND OUT WHERE TO GET A STAMP!

SHORTLY... THIS OLD CLOCKMAKER LOOKS LIKE A GOOD BET! BUT I WON'T BOTHER HIM!...I'LL JUST ENTER HIS MIND WITH MY RING TO GET THE INFORMATION I WANT WITHOUT DISTURBING HIM!

I'M WORRIED...

3

...ABOUT MY FORMER APPRENTICE BITO WLADON WHO LEFT HERE THE OTHER DAY TO GO TO AMERICA! HE'S A BRILLIANT MAN BUT VERY STRANGE! AND HE NEVER CONFIDED IN ME...

eh?

INTENT ON PROBING DEEPER INTO THE CLOCKMAKER'S MEMORY, GREEN LANTERN FINDS HIMSELF DISTRACTED BY THE OLD MAN'S SURFACE THOUGHTS...

BUT YESTERDAY I FOUND THESE NOTES OF WLADON'S...TUCKED AWAY HERE IN THE SHOP...AND THEY FILL ME WITH ALARM! APPARENTLY YOUNG WLADON HAD ALL SORTS OF IDEAS I NEVER KNEW ABOUT...DANGEROUS IDEAS! AND--READING THEM HAS UPSET ME TERRIBLY!

I'VE HEARD TOO MUCH NOT TO FIND OUT WHAT'S IN THOSE NOTES OF THE CLOCKMAKER'S APPRENTICE! IF THEY CONTAIN ANYTHING REALLY DANGEROUS, I OUGHT TO KNOW ABOUT IT...

AT ONCE, THE MYSTIC BEAM, MADE INVISIBLE, DARTS AT THE ASSORTED PAPERS...

GREAT GUARDIANS! IT'S INCREDIBLE--FANTASTIC! IF ONE-HALF OF WHAT'S IN THESE NOTES IS TRUE, I'VE UNCOVERED A MENACE TO THE WHOLE WORLD--I MUST TAKE ACTION WITHOUT DELAY!

IN BRIEF SECONDS, A LITHE EMERALD FIGURE IS ROCKETING ACROSS THE OCEAN...

ACCORDING TO THE THOUGHTS OF THE OLD CLOCKMAKER, THIS APPRENTICE OF HIS-- BITO WLADON--SAILED TO AMERICA-- AND IS ALREADY THERE! I'VE GOT TO GET BACK HOME AS FAST AS POSSIBLE--!

AS THE GREEN GLADIATOR WHIZZES ALONG, HIS OWN MIND IS WORKING...

I CAN'T GET OVER WHAT I READ IN THOSE NOTES! ASTONISHING..!

AT LAST I HAVE DISCOVERED WHAT I AM AFTER...

113

AS SURE AS MY NAME IS *BITO WLADON*, I AM GOING TO PUT MY COUNTRY OF *MODORA* ON THE MAP! FOR TOO LONG IT HAS BEEN IGNORED BY ALL THE OTHER NATIONS OF THE WORLD--THE GREAT AND POWERFUL NATIONS!

I HAVE FIGURED OUT... THAT THE GREATEST NATIONS ON EARTH ARE THOSE WITH THE *MOST POWERFUL WEAPONS!* AT ONE STROKE I SHALL MAKE *MODORA* GREAT BY PROVIDING MY COUNTRY WITH THE *GREATEST WEAPON OF ALL...*

...THE *NUCLEO-SONIC BOMB--A* NEW EXPLOSIVE DEVICE BASED ON *SUPERSONIC ENERGY!* I HAVE DEVOTED MY LIFE TO THE PHENOMENON OF *SOUND* --AND I HAVE BECOME A *MASTER* OF IT! I HAVE MADE SENSATIONAL DISCOVERIES ALREADY...

"FOR INSTANCE, BY MY SCIENCE OF NUCLEO-SONICS I CAN NULLIFY GRAVITY..."

BY GETTING IN TUNE WITH ANY SOUND *SOURCE--* LIKE THAT RADIO, FOR EXAMPLE--MY *NUCLEO-SONIC* MOTOR CAN LIFT ME RIGHT OFF MY FEET!

BY SNAPPING MY ARM AND HAND LIKE A *WHIP*, I CAN SEND OUT A WAVE OF CONCENTRATED *SOUND* THAT KNOCKS OVER A PILE OF BRICKS!

POW!

BUT IN ORDER TO BUILD MY *GREAT WEAPON* I NEED CERTAIN TECHNICAL MATERIALS AVAILABLE ONLY IN A HIGHLY- DEVELOPED COUNTRY LIKE AMERICA! THEREFORE I MUST GO THERE--AND *TAKE* WHAT I NEED!

5

ACCORDING TO THE NOTES, **BITO** REALIZED HE WOULD HAVE TO **STEAL** THE MATERIAL HE NEEDED, BECAUSE IT IS ALL TOP-PRIORITY, CLASSIFIED EQUIPMENT! AND THERE'S ONE OTHER THING I REMEMBER FROM THE NOTES...

"HE DESIGNED HIMSELF A *SPECIAL COSTUME* FOR USE LATER..."

SINCE MY COUNTRY IS ABOUT TO BECOME WORLD-FAMOUS, I MUST BE SUITABLY DRESSED WHEN I APPEAR IN AMERICA! THIS OUTFIT LOOKS RATHER **REGAL**--JUST WHAT I WANT--IN KEEPING WITH THE FUTURE STATUS OF **MODORA!**

BUT I WON'T PUT IT ON UNTIL I REACH THE **U.S.A.!** I DON'T WANT TO AROUSE SUSPICIONS AHEAD OF TIME, IT MIGHT SPOIL EVERY-THING-- ALL THE PLANS FOR MY GREAT MISSION!

AS THE **GREEN-CLAD GLADIATOR** SWEEPS DOWN ON AN EASTERN METROPOLIS...

OF COURSE, I COULD BE KEYED UP FOR NO REASON! THIS **BITO WLADON** MAY BE MERELY A **CRACKPOT** WHOSE IDEAS CAN'T POSSIBLY WORK! BUT HIS NOTES SEEMED SO CONVINCING...

SOON AFTER ON THE STREETS OF THE CITY...

GREAT SCOTT! IT'S **BITO**-- IN HIS SPECIAL COSTUME!

Science
ve Story
SCREEN PLAYS
TOGRAPHY

POST N

SENSATIONAL NE
CRIMINAL STRIKES
AGAIN!

AS **GREEN LANTERN** STARES WIDE-EYED...

"THE MYSTERIOUS THIEF WHOM THE NEWSPAPERS HAVE DUBBED "SONAR"-- BECAUSE OF HIS INCREDIBLE MASTERY OF **SUPERSONIC** SOUND-- LOOTED A HEAVILY-GUARDED U.S. ARSENAL YESTERDAY AND MADE GOOD HIS ESCAPE"...

"SONAR" eh? BITO IS CARRYING OUT HIS **PLAN!**

As the emerald warrior rises to cruise over the city...

According to **Bito's** notes, the material he's after is located in places like arsenals and technical buildings! But how can I cover all the possible sites where he may appear?

I--eh?

Car 37... hurry to Market Square--the Pontex space-laboratory! A robbery--

A space-laboratory!?

That's **exactly** the kind of place where **"Sonar"** would strike for the equipment he wants! I've got to get there fast as I can!

Sure enough, moments later...

There he is!

Djak Lat--!? Who is this hurtling toward me!? Ah! I think I know...

It is none other than the famous crime-fighting champion of the **U.S.A.--Green Lantern!** But he is due now to meet the first complete defeat of his career!

Momentarily setting down his loot--a lead box full of valuable isotopes--on a handy rooftop, Sonar rises for battle...

Coming at me--with his fist poised to strike! Does he think this is going to be a **boxing match?**

My too-confident foe has no idea of the wonders I can perform with my mastery of **sound!**

7

THEN, FANTASTICALLY...

HA! JUST LIKE I CRASHED THAT PILE OF BRICKS BACK IN MY ROOM IN MODORA -- WITH A WHIP-MOTION OF MY FIST -- SENDING OUT A CONCENTRATED BURST OF SUPERSONIC WAVES -- SO I HAVE JUST KNOCKED OUT GREEN LANTERN!

UHH!

AS THE EMERALD-CLAD FIGURE FALLS UNCONSCIOUS TO A NEARBY ROOF...

...HIS GREEN BEAM AUTOMATICALLY SETS UP AN EMERALD SHEATH OF ENERGY AROUND HIM TO PROTECT HIM FROM DESTRUCTION...

AND WHEN THE CRUSADER RECOVERS...

SONAR TOOK ME BY SURPRISE! BUT NEXT TIME WE MEET, THE RESULTS WILL BE DIFFERENT -- I VOW IT -- BY THE GUARDIANS!

THAT AFTERNOON, A HARD-WORKING BALKAN RESTS FROM HIS LABORS...

NATURALLY I DON'T WEAR MY REGAL UNIFORM AROUND THE HOUSE! I KEEP IT ONLY FOR SPECIAL OCCASIONS -- LIKE WHEN I GO OUT TO STEAL! BUT NOW I AM NOT STEALING -- ONLY RESTING!

SO LET ME SEE THE NEWSPAPERS THAT I BOUGHT! OF COURSE I DON'T SPEAK ENGLISH VERY WELL BUT I DO THE BEST THAT I CAN! SO LET ME SEE... HMMMM!

RUSSIA AND AMERICA... AMERICA AND RUSSIA! NOT A SINGLE WORD ABOUT *MODORA*! BUT IT WON'T BE LONG NOW! THINGS ARE GOING TO CHANGE VERY QUICK!

ONE MORE RAID AND I WILL HAVE ALL THE EQUIPMENT I NEED TO BUILD MY *NUCLEO-SONIC* BOMB! AND THEN IT WILL BE MY *BELOVED MODORA* THAT WILL CALL THE TUNE IN THE WORLD! BUT MEANWHILE...

...THIS *GREEN LANTERN* CAN BE A MENACE TO ME! I DEFEATED HIM ONCE...BUT NEXT TIME HE MAY BE READY FOR MY *"SONIC—PUNCH"*! WHAT I NEED IS SOMETHING TO *SURPRISE* HIM WITH! SO LET ME SEE...

LATER, AFTER LONG HOURS OF CONCENTRATED WORK...

I HAVE IT! MY NEW *TUNING FORK GUN*! IT SHOOTS OUT SUPERSONIC VIBRATIONS IN *TUNE* WITH HUMAN BRAIN WAVES...

...AND CREATES THE MOST ASTONISHING *MENTAL EFFECTS*! NOW I AM READY FOR *GREEN LANTERN*! IN FACT, I HOPE HE TRIES TO STOP ME!

HA! HA!

ELSEWHERE IN THE GREAT CITY, A TIRELESS *SEARCHER*...

I'VE SET MY *POWER BEAM* SO THAT AT THE FIRST HINT OF *SONAR*-- AND HIS *SUPERSONIC* TRICKS -- MY RING WILL SIGNAL AN ALARM! BUT SO FAR-- NOT A SIGN...

THEN... MY RING IS REACTING! IT'S POINTING TOWARD THAT BUILDING TO THE NORTH!

STAR ELECTRONIC CO.

LIKE A FIERY GREEN METEOR, THE EMERALD CHAMPION HURTLES TOWARD HIS OBJECTIVE...

SONAR! HE'S COMING OUT WITH LOOT--! THIS TIME I WON'T TAKE ANY CHANCES WITH HIM--!

STAR ELECTRONIC CO.

BUT, THE NEXT MOMENT, SONAR WHIRS OUT HIS TUNING FORK GUN AND...

EH? WHAT'S HE--? BEFORE MY RING COULD REACH HIM--!

QUICK ON THE DRAW, THAT'S ME!

IT'S INCREDIBLE! HOW COULD HE DO THIS? I DON'T UNDERSTAND--!

AROUND THE EMBATTLED GLADIATOR, A STRANGE TRANS-FORMATION...

SONAR--THE STREETS--THE BUILDINGS-- EVERYTHING...HAS TURNED YELLOW! AND--MY RING HAS NO POWER OVER ANYTHING YELLOW--!* I'M FALLING--!

GOODBYE, GREEN LANTERN! MANY UNHAPPY LANDINGS! HA! HA!

*EDITOR'S NOTE: DUE TO A NECESSARY IMPURITY IN THE MATERIAL FROM WHICH IT WAS MADE, GL'S POWER RING HAS NO EFFECT ON ANYTHING YELLOW!

10

TO HIS AMAZEMENT, *GREEN LANTERN* MANAGES TO LAND SAFELY...

THE VERY *AIR* HAS TURNED YELLOW! I CAN'T FLY THROUGH IT!

WITH A TREMENDOUS EFFORT, *GREEN LANTERN* FORCES HIMSELF TO CONSIDER HIS PLIGHT COOLLY...

SONAR COULDN'T HAVE TRANSFORMED *EVERYTHING* THIS WAY! IT MUST BE... THAT HE WORKED THE TRANSFORMATION *THROUGH ME!* SOMEHOW THAT QUEER WEAPON OF HIS HAS AFFECTED MY BRAIN!

IT'S MAKING ME *SEE THINGS YELLOW*... AND THAT IN TURN HAS ACTED ON MY *WILL POWER*... WEAKENING IT! BUT IF I'M RIGHT, THERE OUGHT TO BE A *QUICK WAY* OF GETTING BACK TO NORMAL--

--WITH MY RING!

RING... CLEAR MY HEAD! MAKE ME SEE THINGS AS THEY ARE AGAIN! TAKE AWAY ANY *ILLUSION* THAT HAS BEEN PLACED THERE!

AND A BRIEF MOMENT AFTER, AS THE *POWER BEAM* PERFORMS ITS TASK...

SURE ENOUGH! *SONAR* PUT ME UNDER A KIND OF SPELL! IT GAVE HIM A CHANCE TO GET AWAY!

ONCE AGAIN AN EMERALD LIGHTNING-BOLT CLEAVES THROUGH THE AIR...

BUT HE WON'T GET FAR--!

MEANWHILE, HURTLING EASTWARD ACROSS THE ATLANTIC OCEAN...

I DON'T HAVE TO WORRY ABOUT THAT **GREEN LANTERN**! BY THE TIME HE LOCATES ME AGAIN--IF HE EVER DOES--MY NUCLEAR-SONIC BOMB WILL BE BUILT WITH THIS EQUIPMENT I'VE GOT! AND THEN I WILL DICTATE TERMS TO **EVERYONE**!

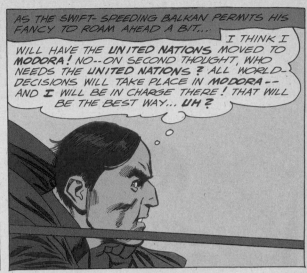

AS THE SWIFT-SPEEDING BALKAN PERMITS HIS FANCY TO ROAM AHEAD A BIT...

I THINK I WILL HAVE THE **UNITED NATIONS** MOVED TO **MODORA**! NO--ON SECOND THOUGHT, WHO NEEDS THE **UNITED NATIONS**? ALL WORLD-DECISIONS WILL TAKE PLACE IN **MODORA**--AND **I** WILL BE IN CHARGE THERE! THAT WILL BE THE BEST WAY... **UH?**

THEN, AS **GREEN LANTERN** ROCKETS INTO VIEW...

GREAT STUFFED GOOSE NECKS!? HOW--!?

THAT TUNING FORK WEAPON OF YOURS LEFT A **FAINT TRAIL** OF RADIATION BEHIND YOU, **SONAR**--ENOUGH FOR MY RING TO DETECT AND FOLLOW!

SO IT LOOKS LIKE YOUR LITTLE TRICK AGAINST ME HAS **BACKFIRED** ON YOU!

YOU CAN'T STOP ME NOW! I--I WON'T PERMIT IT!

BUT THIS TIME WITH DEVASTATING EFFECT THE GREAT GREEN BEAM SHOOTS OUT...

MY **POWER RING** HAS CREATED A **WATERSPOUT** TO TRAP **SONAR**! BUT I'LL RESCUE HIM FROM IT BEFORE HE **DROWNS COMPLETELY**! AND I'LL TAKE HIM TO HIS OWN COUNTRY--THE AUTHORITIES THERE CAN DEAL WITH HIM--AFTER THEY'VE LEARNED ABOUT HIS MAD SCHEME!

G-GAAAHHH!

12

IN DUE COURSE, STRIPPED OF HIS LOOT AND WEAPONS, SONAR IS BEHIND BARS, BUT NOT ALTOGETHER UN-HAPPY...

I'VE PUT MY COUNTRY ON THE MAP! MY EXPLOIT IS IN NEWS-PAPERS ALL OVER THE WORLD!

WHILE ELSEWHERE IN THE TINY NATION...

BY... CAPTURE...OF BITO YOU SAVED... MODORA FROM A DREADFUL ...FATE! NONE OF US WANTS TO RULE THE WORLD, GREEN LANTERN! PLEASE ACCEPT THIS GIFT... AS A TOKEN... OF... OUR GRATEFULNESS...

WHAT COULD BE IN THAT BOX?

A STAMP--A MODORA POSTAGE STAMP!

WE HEARD THAT THIS WAS WHAT... YOU CAME HERE FOR! WE HAD IT PRINTED SPECIALLY FOR YOU!

MUCH LATER, BACK HOME IN COAST CITY...

GOLLY, IT'S GREAT TO BE A PERSONAL FRIEND OF SOMEONE LIKE GREEN LANTERN! HOW ELSE WOULD I BECOME THE ONLY STAMP COLLECTOR ON THE WEST COAST -- MAYBE IN THE WHOLE COUNTRY -- WITH A PRIZE MODORA STAMP IN HIS ALBUM?!

The End

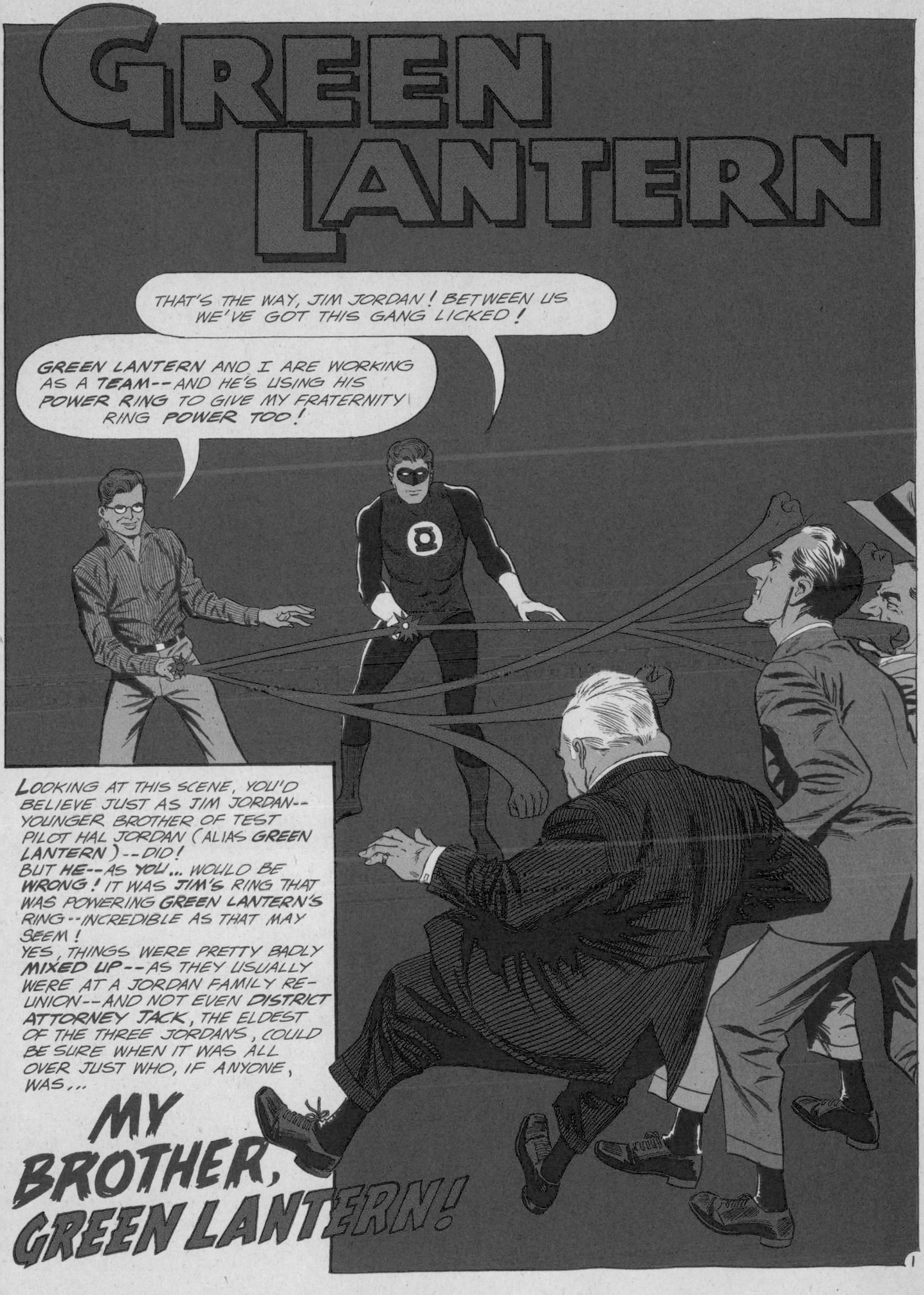
GREEN LANTERN
THAT'S THE WAY, JIM JORDAN! BETWEEN US WE'VE GOT THIS GANG LICKED!
GREEN LANTERN AND I ARE WORKING AS A TEAM--AND HE'S USING HIS POWER RING TO GIVE MY FRATERNITY RING POWER TOO!
LOOKING AT THIS SCENE, YOU'D BELIEVE JUST AS JIM JORDAN--YOUNGER BROTHER OF TEST PILOT HAL JORDAN (ALIAS GREEN LANTERN)--DID! BUT HE--AS YOU... WOULD BE WRONG! IT WAS JIM'S RING THAT WAS POWERING GREEN LANTERN'S RING--INCREDIBLE AS THAT MAY SEEM! YES, THINGS WERE PRETTY BADLY MIXED UP--AS THEY USUALLY WERE AT A JORDAN FAMILY RE-UNION--AND NOT EVEN DISTRICT ATTORNEY JACK, THE ELDEST OF THE THREE JORDANS, COULD BE SURE WHEN IT WAS ALL OVER JUST WHO, IF ANYONE, WAS...
MY BROTHER, GREEN LANTERN!
1

IN HAL JORDAN'S DRESSING ROOM AT THE *FERRIS AIRCRAFT COMPANY*, THE CRACK TEST PILOT REVEALS AN ANNOYING LOSS...

...AND EVERY YEAR AT THIS TIME, PIE, MY BROTHERS JACK AND JIM AND I MEET TO ATTEND OUR COLLEGE FRATERNITY REUNION! AND WE *ALWAYS* WEAR OUR IDENTICAL FRATERNITY RINGS! IT'S TRADITION! ONLY I *CAN'T FIND* MINE...!

SOMEHOW I'VE MISLAID IT! I DON'T KNOW *WHERE* IT IS!

JUMPING FISHHOOKS, HAL! I CAN SOLVE THAT PROBLEM FOR YOU!

AS THOMAS (PIEFACE) KALMAKU, HAL'S ESKIMO GREASEMONKEY, AND LOYAL CONFIDANT, MAKES A GRINNING SUGGESTION...

ALL YOU'VE GOT TO DO IS WEAR YOUR *POWER RING* -- JUST TRANSFORM ITS APPEARANCE FOR THAT DAY INTO YOUR FRATERNITY RING -- AND NO ONE WILL BE THE WISER, GET ME?

PIE, YOU'RE A *GENIUS*! THAT'S EXACTLY WHAT I'LL DO!

AT THE HOME OF JACK JORDAN, ELDEST OF THE JORDAN BROTHERS, NEAR *COAST CITY*...

I'M GLAD TO SEE WE'RE ALL WEARING OUR FRATERNITY RINGS!

ONE FOR ALL AND ALL FOR ONE!

THIS *IS* A BIT WHIMSICAL...

...BUT SINCE JACK AND JIM SEEM TO VALUE OUR FRATERNITY TRADITIONS, I'M GLAD TO KEEP THEM -- FOR THEIR SAKE!

AS USUAL WE'LL GO HUNTING THIS AFTERNOON...

...AND THEN COME BACK IN TIME TO GET READY FOR THE REUNION THIS EVENING!

SWELL! LEAD THE WAY, JACK!

♪ A MIGHTY HUNTER WAS HE! ♪

2

BUT UNKNOWN TO THE THREE SPORTSMEN AS THEY HEAD FOR THE WOODS...

--HELLO!

THERE DOESN'T SEEM TO BE ANY-BODY HOME!

HELLO!

A MOMENT LATER...

WHERE *IS* EVERYBODY? I WAS IN THE NEIGH-BORHOOD--WORKING ON A STORY FOR MY MAGAZINE, *BEHIND THE SCENES*--AND I THOUGHT I'D DROP IN ON MY BOY FRIEND, JIM JORDAN!* BUT THIS IS A FINE WELCOME, I MUST SAY--!

Editor's Note: THE CIRCUMSTANCES UNDER WHICH SUE WILLIAMS MET--AND FELL IN LOVE WITH-- JIM JORDAN WERE REVEALED IN *"GREEN LANTERN'S BROTHER ACT "*-- IN THE DECEMBER, 1961 ISSUE OF *GREEN LANTERN!*

AS PRETTY SUE WILLIAMS, WITHOUT ANY ADO, MAKES HERSELF AT HOME...

I'LL WAIT FOR JIM! HE CAN'T BE FAR AWAY! HE DOESN'T GO TO WORK OR ANYTHING! AND ALSO...I MUST REMEMBER TO TELL HIS BROTHER JACK TO *LOCK THE DOOR* WHEN THERE'S NO ONE HERE! AFTER ALL...

chocolates

...I MIGHT HAVE BEEN A *BURGLAR* OR SOMETHING! AND IT WOULDN'T HELP THAT *JACK JORDAN* IS *DISTRICT ATTORNEY*--HE COULD STILL BE ROBBED! er-- WAIT! THAT DOES GIVE ME AN IDEA, THOUGH!

SUDDENLY, SUE IS IN ACTION...

FOR WEEKS I'VE BEEN WANTING TO GET A LOOK AT *JIM JORDAN'S* ROOM WHILE HE'S NOT THERE! IF I'M RIGHT, IT MAY HELP ME PROVE MY THEORY THAT HE *IS REALLY GREEN LANTERN!* AND *NOW* IS MY CHANCE!

THEN...

GOOD GOSH--LOOKY THERE! I'LL BET A MILLION DOLLARS-- THAT'S *GREEN LANTERN'S* FAMOUS *POWER BATTERY!* AT LAST I'VE GOT THE GOODS ON CLEVER MR. *"HAPPY-GO-LUCKY"* JIM JORDAN!

3

MEANWHILE IN THE NEARBY WOODS...

BOY, ALL I BAGGED WAS A GOOD CASE OF POISON IVY!

WE'D BETTER GET YOU TO A DOCTOR, HAL!

SOON, IN TOWN...

NO, IT'S NOT SERIOUS! I'LL JUST TREAT IT AND YOU'LL BE ALL RIGHT IN A FEW HOURS! TAKE OFF YOUR RING, MR. JORDAN!

TAKE OFF... MY RING?

YES, SO I CAN SWAB DOWN YOUR ENTIRE HAND!

er--OF COURSE! SURE THING, DOCTOR!

I MUSN'T MAKE A FUSS OR MY BROTHERS WILL SUSPECT THERE'S SOMETHING ABOUT MY RING!

THEN...

IT JUST FEELS ODD LETTING MY DISGUISED POWER RING OUT OF MY POSSESSION EVEN FOR A MOMENT--

BETTER HAVE A LOOK AT MY HAND TOO, DOC!

I THINK I'VE GOT A TOUCH OF POISON IVY, ALSO!

JIM WOULD COMPLICATE THINGS! BUT I'VE GOT MY EYES GLUED ON MY RING! I WOULDN'T WANT...

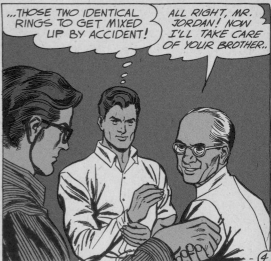

...THOSE TWO IDENTICAL RINGS TO GET MIXED UP BY ACCIDENT!

ALL RIGHT, MR. JORDAN! NOW I'LL TAKE CARE OF YOUR BROTHER..

-4-

BACK HOME, SHORTLY AFTERWARD..

WE STILL HAVE TWO HOURS BEFORE THE REUNION! THAT WILL GIVE US ALL A CHANCE TO REST UP...

JACK HAS EVERYTHING WORKED OUT ACCORDING TO SCHEDULE..

ALL RIGHT, IF I HAVE TO REST, I SUPPOSE I HAVE TO!

SEE YOU LATER!

BUT IN THE ROOM OF THE YOUNGEST OF THE THREE BROTHERS, A MOMENT LATER..

SUE! YOU! HERE--!?

YES, I AM MR. JORDAN! WAITING PATIENTLY TO TELL YOU--

I'VE FOUND YOUR POWER BATTERY-- SO NOW YOU MIGHT AS WELL STOP THE MASQUERADE-- AND ADMIT OPENLY TO ME THAT YOU'RE GREEN LANTERN!

M-MY POWER BATTERY--!?

SUE, YOU KNOW MY HOBBY IS OLD SPORTS CARS! THAT'S A LAMP FROM A FABULOUS ANTIQUE AUTO--THE 1904 BERCEDES-- MENZ, THE ONLY ONE OF ITS KIND! I FOUND THE LAMP AT A JUNK DEALER...

HAR-DE-HAR-HAR-HAR! YOU EXPECT ME TO BELIEVE THAT?

I SUPPOSE YOU'LL EVEN INSIST THAT RING YOU'RE WEARING IS NOT YOUR POWER RING IN DISGUISE! Hmmph! MAYBE YOU CAN FOOL OTHERS, JIM JORDAN--BUT NOT SUE WILLIAMS!

WOO-EE! SHE'S GOT ME HALF-CONVINCED!

I MIGHT AS WELL MAKE A GAG OUT OF THIS—JUST FOR KICKS!

OKAY, SUE! YOU WIN! er—MIND IF I CHARGE MY RING NOW THAT YOU KNOW MY SECRET?

BE MY GUEST!

IN BRIGHTEST DAY, IN BLACKEST NIGHT, NO EVIL SHALL ... SAY, WHAT COMES NEXT, SUE?

ALWAYS THE GAGSTER! OH, WELL...

"...SHALL ESCAPE MY SIGHT!"

AFTER THE "RING" HAS BEEN "RECHARGED"...

NOW HOW ABOUT A PRIVATE DEMONSTRATION, GL! LET'S SEE YOU WILL—POWER THE RING TO FLY YOU UP TO THE CEILING!

ALL RIGHT! RING.. YOU HEARD THE LADY! FLY ME UP TO THE CEILING!

THE NEXT MOMENT, ASTONISHINGLY...

GREAT JUMPING JUPITER!?

BRAVO!

BUT THEN...

WELL, THAT'S CLUMSY! JIM'S SMACKED HIS HEAD AGAINST THE CEILING—! HE WILLED HIS RING TO FLY HIM UP TO THE CEILING ALL RIGHT—BUT THEN NEGLECTED TO COMMAND THE RING TO STOP HIS UPWARD FLIGHT IN TIME!

THE POOR DARLING'S KNOCKED HIMSELF COLD! I'D BETTER FIND HIS BROTHER JACK! BUT... I MUST BE CAREFUL NOT TO GIVE AWAY JIM'S SECRET...!

AS SUE LEAVES THE ROOM...

THE COAST IS CLEAR, MOOSE! C'MON!

IT'S THE LAMP, ALL RIGHT! THERE WAS ONLY *TWO* MADE LIKE THAT...

THE TWO MEN CAUTIOUSLY ENTER THE ROOM...

...AND MR. BLACKSTREET'S ALREADY GOT THE OTHER ONE!

HEY--IT'S *EMPTY!* MOOSE, WE GOTTA WORK FAST! GRAB THAT GUY--WE'RE TAKING HIM WITH US!

BUT I TELL YOU JIM WAS RIGHT HERE--AND HE WAS UNCONSCIOUS! HE--er--HIT HIS HEAD!

HUSTLE!

WELL, HE'S NOT HERE NOW, SUE!

THAT BLACK SEDAN--TAKING OFF FROM NEAR THE HOUSE!?

er--I'D BETTER HAVE A LOOK AROUND THE GROUNDS, JACK...

AND INSTANTS LATER...

JIM COULD BE IN REAL TROUBLE!

I HAD TO GET AWAY FROM THE OTHERS BACK IN THE HOUSE, IN ORDER TO *CHANGE* TO *GREEN LANTERN*--AND GO AFTER THAT *CAR!*

BUT AS THE *EMERALD GLADIATOR* SETS HIMSELF TO ZOOM OFF IN HOT PURSUIT...

UH--SOMETHING SEEMS TO HAVE GONE WRONG WITH MY *POWER RING!* I--I'M STANDING STILL! I'M *NOT MOVING* AT ALL--!

⑦

I KNOW I CHARGED MY RING THIS MORNING, SO IT CAN'T--*er*, WAIT A SECOND! I WONDER... THERE'S ONLY *ONE* POSSIBLE WAY TO EXPLAIN THIS FANTASTIC OCCURRENCE! MY BROTHER JIM AND I...

...MUST HAVE *SWITCHED RINGS* BACK IN THAT DOCTOR'S OFFICE! I THOUGHT I TOOK *MY RING* BACK... BUT I MUST HAVE TAKEN *HIS!* GREAT GUARDIANS--! BUT I'VE STILL GOT A CHANCE TO TRAIL THAT CAR--BY USING JIM'S SPORTS CAR!

BEREFT OF HIS MYSTIC BEAM, THE CRACK TEST PILOT PUTS HIS LIGHTNING REFLEXES TO WORK...

OF COURSE IT WILL SEEM ODD IF *GREEN LANTERN* IS SEEN DRIVING JIM JORDAN'S CAR... BUT I'VE GOT TO RISK IT! THERE'S THE SEDAN...I'VE MANAGED TO KEEP IT IN VIEW...!

HALF AN HOUR LATER...

THEY'RE TURNING INTO THAT DRIVEWAY! I'D BETTER PULL INTO THIS TREE-COVERED LANE!

HE'S COMING TO, MOOSE! WATCH HIM--!

AND SOON, INSIDE THE HOUSE...

THE LAMP WAS EMPTY, MR. BLACKSTREET-- SO WE BROUGHT JORDAN ALONG! HE MUST HAVE THE ICE--

I MUST HAVE... WHAT ICE!?

SAY, WHAT IS THIS ALL ABOUT? WHERE AM I?

PLEASE BE GOOD ENOUGH TO SIT DOWN, MR. JORDAN, AND I WILL BE HAPPY TO EXPLAIN! YES, BY JOVE! SIT DOWN, SIR...

130

YOU'RE YOUNG, MR. JORDAN, SO OF COURSE YOU WOULDN'T RECALL THAT MOST FABULOUS CRIME OF THE YEAR 1912 --THE THEFT OF THE ARCH-DUKE'S *BLUE DIAMOND*, THE GREATEST STONE OF ITS KIND IN HISTORY! AH YES, WHAT A STONE! THERE WERE *TWO* THIEVES ...

...AND THEY MADE THEIR ESCAPE --A NOVEL IDEA AT THE TIME --IN AN AUTO, A 1904 BERCEDES-MENZ! AFTERWARDS, THE TWO WERE CAP-TURED, BUT THE JEWEL WAS NEVER FOUND! IT HAD VANISHED COMPLETELY! MUCH LATER, I STUDIED THE CASE! I FOUND IT FASCINATING, SIR...

AND I DEVELOPED A THEORY! I BECAME CONVINCED THAT THE ARCHDUKE'S DIAMOND HAD BEEN HIDDEN SOMEWHERE IN THE GET-AWAY CAR! DO YOU FOLLOW ME, SIR? DOWN THROUGH THE YEARS I HAVE BEEN ON THE TRAIL OF THE JEWEL! I HAVE HAD AGENTS WORKING FOR ME ...

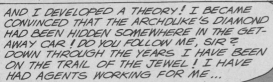

I HAVE SPENT UNTOLD SUMS! AH, YES! AND IN DUE COURSE I ASSEM-BLED EVERY PIECE OF THAT OLD ORIGINAL BERCEDES-MENZ FROM JUNKYARDS IN THE FOUR CORNERS OF THE COUNTRY! LET ME SHOW YOU, SIR...

THE 1904 BERCEDES-MENZ!!

YES! BUT I DID *NOT* FIND THE DIAMOND! UP UNTIL TODAY THE ONLY PIECE MISSING HAS BEEN THIS LAMP IN YOUR POSSESSION, MR. JORDAN! I WAS CONFIDENT IT *MUST* CONTAIN THE JEWEL! YOU SEE, MY INTENSIVE RESEARCH PROVED NO ONE ELSE HAD FOUND IT ...

THEREFORE, SIR, YOU WILL OBLIGE ME BY HANDING OVER THE GEM! THE ONLY REMAINING POSSIBILITY IS THAT YOU REMOVED THE ARCHDUKE'S DIAMOND FROM THIS LAMP BEFORE MY MEN GOT TO IT!

I-- GULP!? ME-- GULP?!

AT THAT MOMENT...

I'VE HEARD ENOUGH-- AND I'VE FIGURED OUT HOW TO USE MY POWER RING THAT JIM IS WEARING-- WITHOUT AROUSING HIS SUSPICIONS! BUT I CAN'T DELAY AN INSTANT LONGER...

BY JOVE! IT'S GREEN LANTERN!

FROM A FEW FEET AWAY I CAN OPERATE MY RING MENTALLY, BY SHEER FORCE OF WILL! I KNOW IT CAN WORK BECAUSE I ONCE DID IT!* AND THAT'S MY IDEA NOW...

*Editor's Note: IN THE "WINGS OF DESTINY" STORY WHERE GL IN A DREAM TURNED HIS FRIEND PIEFACE INTO A BIRD!

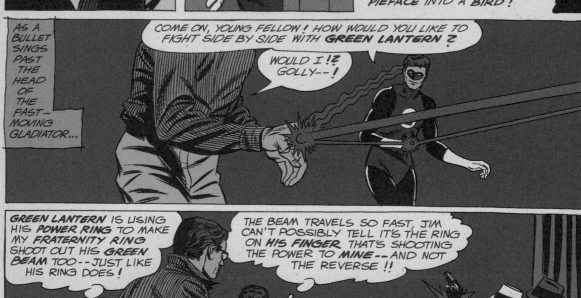

AS A BULLET SINGS PAST THE HEAD OF THE FAST-MOVING GLADIATOR...

COME ON, YOUNG FELLOW! HOW WOULD YOU LIKE TO FIGHT SIDE BY SIDE WITH GREEN LANTERN?

WOULD I!? GOLLY--!

GREEN LANTERN IS USING HIS POWER RING TO MAKE MY FRATERNITY RING SHOOT OUT HIS GREEN BEAM TOO-- JUST LIKE HIS RING DOES!

THE BEAM TRAVELS SO FAST, JIM CAN'T POSSIBLY TELL IT'S THE RING ON HIS FINGER THAT'S SHOOTING THE POWER TO MINE-- AND NOT THE REVERSE!!

THE NEXT INSTANT...

THIS IS TERRIFIC! OUR RINGS HAVE FORMED MULTIPLE FISTS THAT ARE ATTACKING THAT GANG AND KNOCKING THEM OUT!

I'VE STILL GOT TO **SWITCH** RINGS BACK WITH JIM...!

SOON, WITH BLACKSTREET AND HIS MINIONS **HORS DE COMBAT**...

NICE GOING! WE MAKE QUITE A TEAM, JIM JORDAN!

WHAT A MARVEL **GREEN LANTERN** IS! HE KNOWS MY NAME--HE TURNS UP HERE IN THE NICK OF TIME--

YOU'D BETTER LET ME "**CLEAN**" YOUR RING! WORKING TOGETHER THE WAY WE DID, MY GREEN BEAM MAY HAVE LEFT SOME **STRONG RADIATION** ON YOUR RING, BUT I'LL FIX IT...

SURE! HERE YOU ARE, GL...

THEN...

UHH--THAT LIGHT!

BLINDING HIM FOR A MOMENT...! BUT A MOMENT IS ALL I NEED...

...TO SWITCH RINGS AGAIN WITHOUT HIS KNOWING IT!

er--THERE YOU ARE, JIM! YOUR RING'S FINE NOW!

GOLLY!

LATER, WITH THE GANG UNDER ARREST...

...AND HERE IS THE FAMOUS "ARCHDUKE" DIAMOND, SERGEANT! USING MY RING I LOCATED IT... CLEVERLY WEDGED IN THE BOTTOM OF THIS LAMP!

EGAD!

I WAS RIGHT, BY JOVE! THE DIAMOND WAS HIDDEN IN THE BERCEDES—MENZ!

YOU'VE SOLVED A SIXTY-YEAR-OLD CRIME-PUZZLE, GREEN LANTERN!

AS JIM JORDAN SEEKS TO DUPLICATE A POWER-RING PERFORMANCE...

I CAN'T GET OFF THE GROUND! HMM! I GUESS MY FLYING UP TO THE CEILING WAS A FREAK STUNT--CAUSED BY SHEER WILL-POWER!

PLAYING COY AGAIN, PRETENDING HE ISN'T GREEN LANTERN! BUT I KNOW BETTER!

AND THAT NIGHT...

ONE FOR ALL AND ALL FOR ONE!

I GUESS FRATERNITY REUNIONS CAN BE PRETTY EXCITING AFTER ALL ... ESPECIALLY A REUNION OF THE THREE JORDAN BROTHERS!

The End

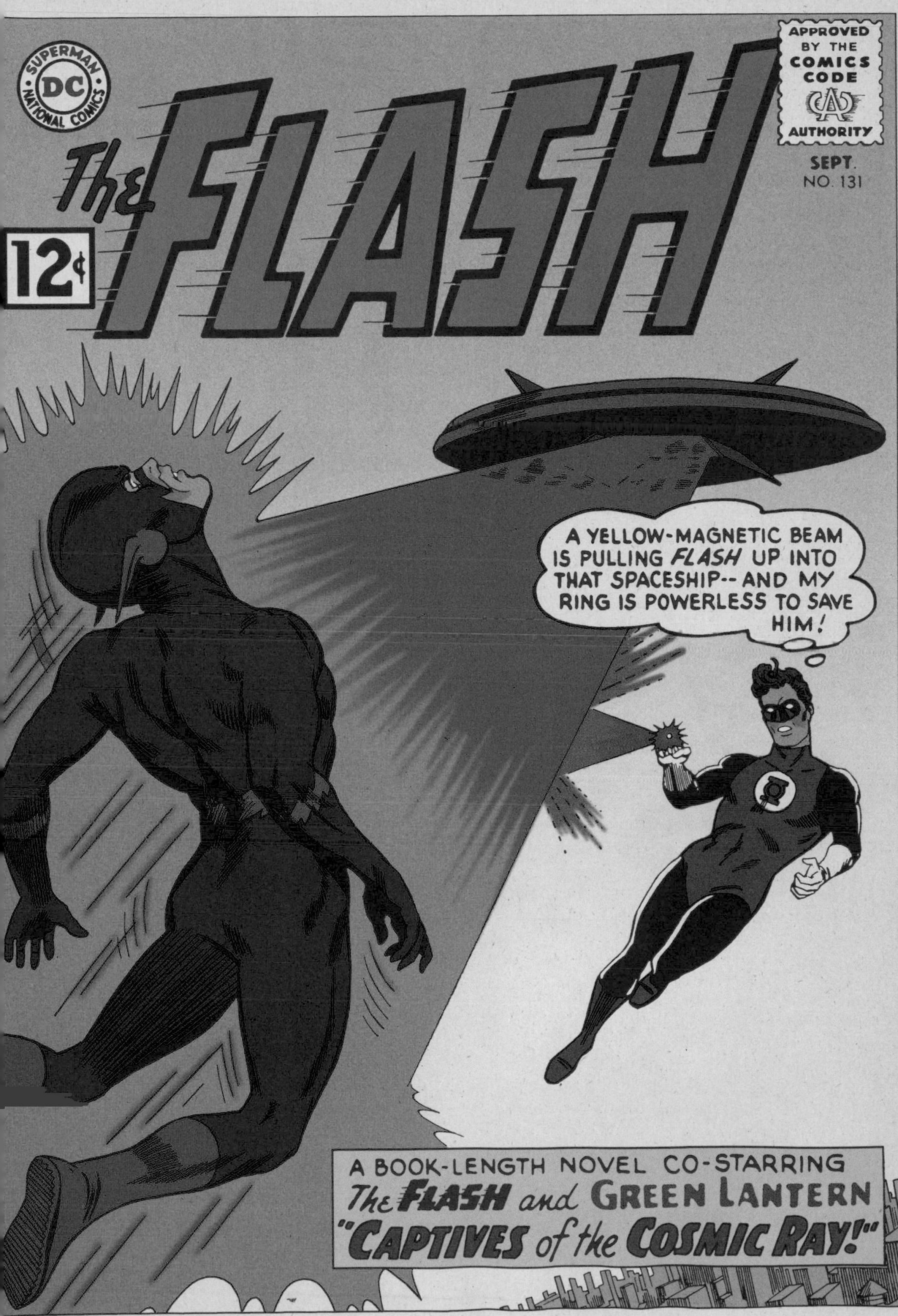
SUPERMAN DC NATIONAL COMICS
APPROVED BY THE COMICS CODE AUTHORITY
The FLASH
12¢
SEPT.
NO. 131
A YELLOW-MAGNETIC BEAM IS PULLING FLASH UP INTO THAT SPACESHIP-- AND MY RING IS POWERLESS TO SAVE HIM!
A BOOK-LENGTH NOVEL CO-STARRING
The FLASH and GREEN LANTERN
"CAPTIVES of the COSMIC RAY!"

THE FLASH

CAPTIVES OF THE COSMIC RAY!

LIKE CHINESE BOXES, IT WAS A PUZZLE INSIDE A PUZZLE!

WHY HAD **FLASH** BEEN TRANSPORTED TO A FAR-OFF **PLANET** OF **MYSTERY?**

AND AFTER *GREEN LANTERN,* SEEKING TO HELP, FOLLOWED HIM -- WHAT WAS THE MEANING OF THE STRANGE ATTACKS ON THE FAMOUS PAIR THERE? BUT THE GREATEST SURPRISE OF ALL -- AND THE GREATEST SHOCK -- STILL AWAITED THE TWO SUPER-HEROES WHEN THEY BECAME ...

THE MOUNTAIN ON THIS STRANGE PLANET -- IT'S **COME ALIVE** -- SEIZING HOLD OF **GREEN LANTERN** AND ME!

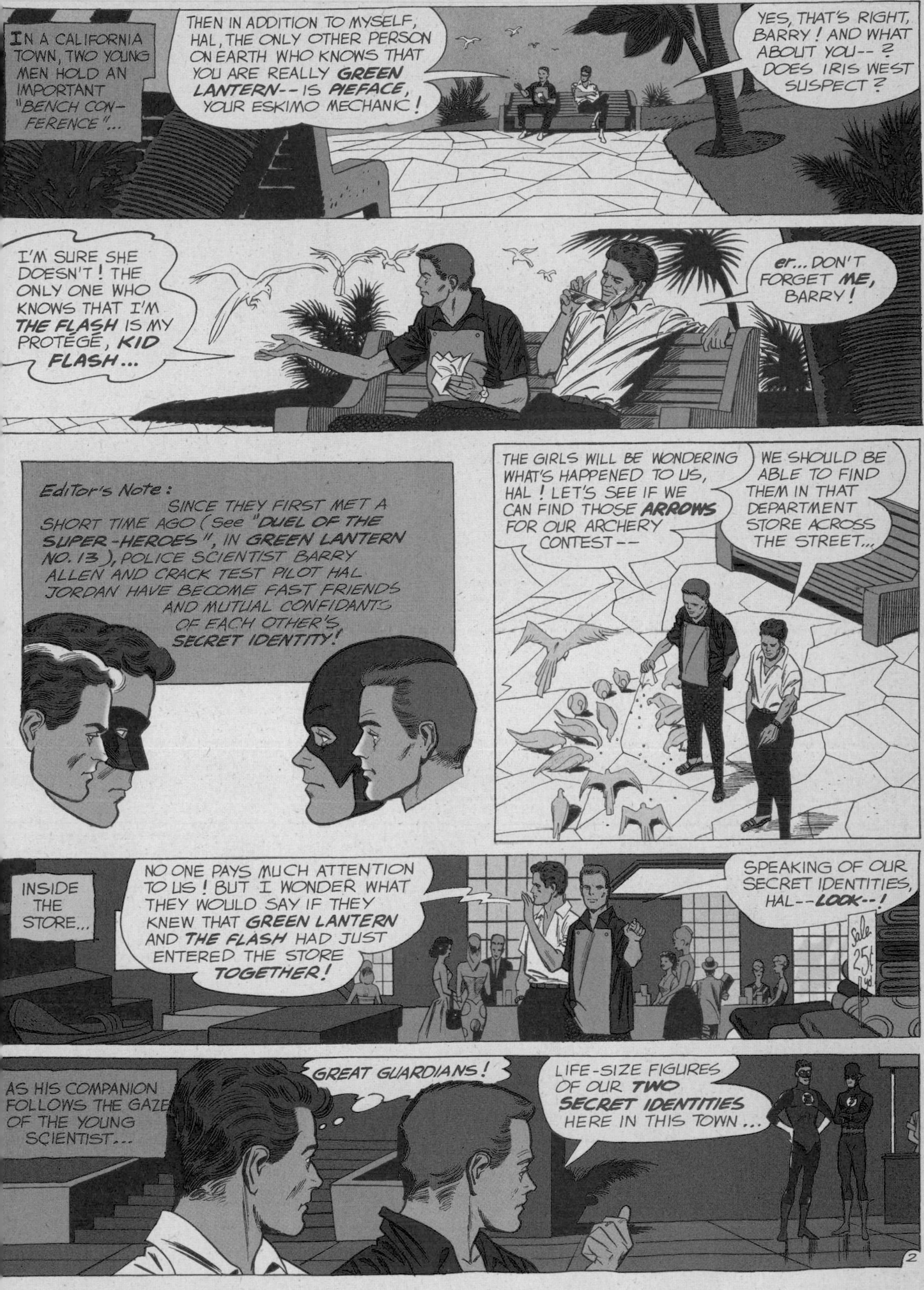
IN A CALIFORNIA TOWN, TWO YOUNG MEN HOLD AN IMPORTANT "BENCH CON-FERENCE"...
THEN IN ADDITION TO MYSELF, HAL, THE ONLY OTHER PERSON ON EARTH WHO KNOWS THAT YOU ARE REALLY GREEN LANTERN-- IS PIEFACE, YOUR ESKIMO MECHANIC!
YES, THAT'S RIGHT, BARRY! AND WHAT ABOUT YOU--? DOES IRIS WEST SUSPECT?
I'M SURE SHE DOESN'T! THE ONLY ONE WHO KNOWS THAT I'M THE FLASH IS MY PROTÉGÉ, KID FLASH...
er... DON'T FORGET ME, BARRY!
Editor's Note: SINCE THEY FIRST MET A SHORT TIME AGO (See "DUEL OF THE SUPER-HEROES", IN GREEN LANTERN NO. 13), POLICE SCIENTIST BARRY ALLEN AND CRACK TEST PILOT HAL JORDAN HAVE BECOME FAST FRIENDS AND MUTUAL CONFIDANTS OF EACH OTHER'S SECRET IDENTITY!
THE GIRLS WILL BE WONDERING WHAT'S HAPPENED TO US, HAL! LET'S SEE IF WE CAN FIND THOSE ARROWS FOR OUR ARCHERY CONTEST--
WE SHOULD BE ABLE TO FIND THEM IN THAT DEPARTMENT STORE ACROSS THE STREET...
INSIDE THE STORE...
NO ONE PAYS MUCH ATTENTION TO US! BUT I WONDER WHAT THEY WOULD SAY IF THEY KNEW THAT GREEN LANTERN AND THE FLASH HAD JUST ENTERED THE STORE TOGETHER!
SPEAKING OF OUR SECRET IDENTITIES, HAL--LOOK--!
Sale 25¢ yd.
AS HIS COMPANION FOLLOWS THE GAZE OF THE YOUNG SCIENTIST...
GREAT GUARDIANS!
LIFE-SIZE FIGURES OF OUR TWO SECRET IDENTITIES HERE IN THIS TOWN...
2

NOW *THAT'S* AN APPEAL *I* CAN'T RESIST, HAL!

FLASH AND GREEN LANTERN SUPPORT NATIONAL CHARITIES FOR ORPHANS!

HAVE *YOU* CONTRIBUTED YET?

ME NEITHER, BARRY!

THANK YOU, GENTLEMEN!

LATER AT THE ESTATE OF CAROL FERRIS, HAL'S PRETTY BOSS, NEAR THE TOWN...

HERE THEY ARE!

WELL IT'S ABOUT TIME! WHERE HAVE YOU TWO BEEN?

WE'VE BEEN DOING SOME ARROW-SHOPPING AND--*er*--SEEING THE SIGHTS!

PIEFACE, HAL AND I ARE NOW READY TO DECIDE WHICH OF US IS THE *SPORTS CHAMPION* OF THIS WEEK-END!

GREAT! I'VE GOT THE TARGET ALL SET UP!

IT'S EXACTLY EVEN BETWEEN THEM SO FAR, ISN'T IT, THOMAS?

YES, CAROL! BARRY HAS BEATEN HAL IN TENNIS AND SWIMMING...

...WHILE HAL HAS BEATEN BARRY IN GOLF AND BILLIARDS! THIS ARCHERY MATCH WILL DECIDE THE WINNER!

FIVE ARROWS APIECE, RIGHT?

RIGHTO!

3

AS THE TWO CONTESTANTS PREPARE TO "SHOOT IT OUT"...

THAT *HIGH-PITCHED* WHINE! I'VE NEVER HEARD ANYTHING SO *ODD!* WHAT--?

IT'S COMING CLOSER-- WHATEVER IT IS!

EEEEEEE!

THE NEXT MOMENT, AN UNEARTHLY VESSEL BURSTS INTO VIEW...

DOWN, EVERYBODY! *DOWN!*

LIKE A GIANT SCYTHE THE ALIEN SHIP FLATTENS EVERYTHING UNDER IT...

ITS EXHAUST-- THROWING OFF HEAT-BLASTS AS IT PASSES BY--

HAL, ARE YOU THINKING WHAT I AM?

I SURE AM, BARRY! AND LET'S NOT WASTE ANY TIME!

SOON, INSIDE A CONVENIENT GARAGE...

WHAT HAPPENED TO HAL AND BARRY?

THEY MUST HAVE DASHED AFTER THAT AMAZING SHIP--TO KEEP IT IN VIEW, I GUESS!

THE UNIFORM SPURTING FROM THE RING ON BARRY ALLEN'S FINGER EXPANDS SWIFTLY ON CONTACT WITH THE AIR! AND MOMENTS LATER... TWO FAMILIAR EYE-CATCHING FIGURES ARE HURTLING ALONG SIDE BY SIDE...

IT WENT TOWARD *COAST CITY,* FLASH!

LET'S GO, *GREEN LANTERN!* WE'VE GOT TO FIND OUT WHAT THAT SHIP IS UP TO!

4

SPLIT-SECONDS LATER IN THE NEARBY METROPOLIS...

I'LL NEED MORE **WILL POWER** IF I'M GOING TO KEEP UP WITH **FLASH'S SUPER-SPEED!**

THERE IT IS!

BUT THE NEXT MOMENT, INCREDIBLY...

A **YELLOW** BEAM HAS SHOT DOWN FROM THE SHIP...AND **FLASH** IS BEING DRAWN UPWARDS HELPLESSLY INSIDE IT! SOMEHOW I MUST FIND A WAY TO SAVE HIM -- EVEN THOUGH MY RING HAS **NO POWER** OVER ANYTHING **YELLOW!** *

*Editor's Note: DUE TO A NECESSARY IMPURITY IN THE MATERIAL FROM WHICH IT IS MADE, GL'S RING CANNOT OPERATE AGAINST **YELLOW!**

THEN, AS THE **SCARLET SPEEDSTER** VANISHES INSIDE THE ALIEN VESSEL WHICH AT ONCE STREAKS OFF AT A FANTASTIC RATE...

IT...MUST BE TRAVELING NEAR THE SPEED OF LIGHT! BUT I WON'T LET IT GET AWAY FROM ME...

SUDDENLY...

IT BLINKED OUT OF SIGHT -- **VANISHED!** IT MUST HAVE BROKEN THROUGH THE **LIGHT-BARRIER!** OKAY -- HERE I GO, TOO!

⑤

SWIFTLY EXCEEDING THE SPEED OF LIGHT HIMSELF BY MEANS OF HIS AMAZING *POWER RING*, GREEN LANTERN SUCCEEDS IN TRAILING THE MYSTERIOUS VESSEL ACROSS THE VOID OF SPACE AND TO AN UNKNOWN PLANET!

THE STRANGE SPACESHIP DROPPED *FLASH* OFF-- AND THEN TOOK OFF AGAIN! I'VE GOT TO KEEP AFTER IT--FIND OUT WHAT GAME IT'S PLAYING!

LIKE GREEN LIGHTNING, THE *EMERALD GLADIATOR* ZOOMS AFTER HIS QUARRY, RING BLAZING...

SNARED IT! I'M OVERCOMING ITS TREMENDOUS DRIVE-FORCE-- AND BRINGING IT TO A STAND-STILL!

BACKING HIS MYSTIC BEAM WITH HIS INDOMITABLE WILL POWER, *GREEN LANTERN* SWIFTLY BEARS THE SHIP TO THE GROUND...

I'VE WEIGHED THE SHIP DOWN--WITH ENERGY-WEIGHTS CREATED BY MY RING--WHERE IT'LL STAY PUT WHILE I BREAK IN AND DEAL WITH WHO-EVER'S INSIDE IT!

I DON'T SEE ANY DOORS OR HATCHES! BUT, THANKS TO MY RING I DON'T NEED ANY ENTRANCE! I CAN *MAKE MY OWN!*

GRIMLY READY, THE AROUSED CRUSADER CONFRONTS A SURPRISING SITUATION A MOMENT LATER...

HUH--? NO ONE HERE! THIS SHIP IS EMPTY! IT'S RUN COM-PLETELY BY *MACHINERY!*

SOMEHOW... I FEEL I'VE BEEN LED ASTRAY... INTO A *TRAP!* I'D BETTER GET OUT OF HERE -- HURRY BACK AND SEE HOW *FLASH* IS MAKING OUT!

SOME DISTANCE AWAY, THE CRIMSON-CLAD CRUSADER FINDS HIMSELF IN A STRANGE PREDICAMENT...

I SPIED *GREEN LANTERN* AND STARTED TO FOLLOW HIM--WHEN THIS BLINDING, WHIRLING SNOWSTORM SPRANG UP AROUND ME! I--I'VE LOST ALL SENSE OF DIRECTION!

7

142

THEN, SUDDENLY OUT OF THE SNOWSTORM AN AWESOME SHAPE COALESCES...

UHH? THAT GIANT CREATURE... FORMING OUT OF THE SNOW... AND ADVANCING ON ME --!

AS A WAVE OF COLD FROM THE "ABOMINABLE SNOWMAN" STRIKES *FLASH,* SLOWING DOWN HIS SUPER-SWIFT REFLEXES...

ALMOST GRABBED ME! THE COLD COMING FROM IT IS OVERWHELMING -- NUMBING! I'VE GOT TO WARM UP -- OR IT WILL FINISH ME!

BEFORE DISASTER CAN OVERCOME HIM, THE *SULTAN OF SPEED* FINDS AN ANSWER...

VIBRATION! BY SUPER-SPEED I CAN VIBRATE THE ATOMS INSIDE MY BODY A MILLION TIMES A SECOND! IF THAT DOESN'T WARM ME UP, NOTHING WILL!

THAWED OUT IN MOMENTS, *FLASH* MAKES SHORT WORK OF HIS OUTSIZED ADVERSARY...

UNDER THE TITANIC GUSTS OF WIND I'M SPINNING AT IT, THE CREATURE IS BURSTING APART -- LIKE SNOW BLOWN FROM A TREE BACK HOME!

ABRUPTLY, THE NEXT MOMENT...

THE STORM VANISHED AS SUDDENLY AS IT BEGAN! DOES THIS MEAN THE DANGER IS OVER, OR--? WHAT'S THAT BEHIND ME?

ANOTHER ALIEN BEING THREATENING ME! BUT I-- I CAN SEE RIGHT THROUGH HIM!

TRUE! I AM ONLY A PROJECTED ENERGY IMAGE, FLASH! BUT THAT WILL NOT PREVENT ME FROM DESTROYING YOU!

THEN, FANTASTICALLY, BEFORE THE SUPER-SWIFT SPEEDSTER CAN EVEN MAKE A MOVE...

A BOLT OF FORCE FROM THAT WEAPON--TURNED ME UPSIDE DOWN! AND NOW NO MATTER HOW HARD I TRY, I CAN'T RIGHT MYSELF -- CAN'T GET MY FEET DOWN ON THE GROUND!

THAT'S JUST TO TIRE YOU OUT-- AND SLOW YOU DOWN SO YOU CAN'T ESCAPE ME!

AND NOW FOR MY FINAL COUP-- THIS NEXT SHOT WILL ELIMINATE YOU FOREVER AS OUR ENEMY!

*Editor's Note: BY HIS UNCANNY SWIFTNESS, FLASH CAN GET AS MUCH PRACTICE IN A SPLIT-SECOND AS AN ORDINARY PERSON IN YEARS!

BY MOVING SUPER-SPEEDILY, FLASH'S FEET ARE GIVING OFF ENERGY-VIBRATIONS THAT CLASH WITH AND ACT TO DESTROY THE BODILESS IMAGE HE IS UP AGAINST!

MEANWHILE, ON HIS WAY TOWARD *THE FLASH*, *GREEN LANTERN* TOO' HAS MET STRANGE OPPOSITION ...

SUDDENLY THE *GRAVITY* AROUND ME SEEMS TO HAVE INCREASED A HUNDRED-FOLD! IT'S PULLING ME DOWN AT ACCELERATING SPEED--!

CAN'T STOP MY DESCENT... THE FORCE OF GRAVITY SEEMS STRONGER THAN THAT OF MY *POWER RING!* GOING TO CRASH HARD--

--UNLESS I *CUSHION MY FALL*--BY POWER-RINGING A BED-SPRING MATTRESS UNDERNEATH ME ...!

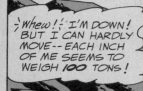

;*Whew!*; I'M DOWN! BUT I CAN HARDLY MOVE-- EACH INCH OF ME SEEMS TO WEIGH *100* TONS!

AND THEN, WITH THE GREEN-GARBED WARRIOR NEARLY HELPLESS...

A RIVER OF *MOLTEN METAL*-- BURSTING DOWN DIRECTLY AT ME FROM THAT HILL-- SETTING FIRE TO EVERYTHING ALONG ITS COURSE ...!

WITH A TREMENDOUS SURGE OF WILL POWER, THE DAUNTLESS CRUSADER SUCCEEDS IN RAISING HIMSELF FROM THE GROUND JUST IN TIME BY *REACTION-PROPULSION*, AS HIS MIGHTY GREEN BEAM BECOMES A MULTI-STAGED ROCKET UNDER HIM...

I MANAGED TO LIFT OFF--AND NOT A MOMENT TOO SOON! THE HEAT FROM THAT LIQUID METAL IS ALMOST SUFFOCATING ME!

MOMENTS LATER...

THE GRAVITY IS BACK TO NORMAL--AS SUDDENLY AS IT INCREASED! I CAN FLY AGAIN--!

AND SOON AFTER...

FLASH! ARE YOU ALL RIGHT?

YES! AND YOU, *GREEN LANTERN*--? I WAS AFRAID--

AFTER THE TWO CHAMPIONS HAVE EXCHANGED ACCOUNTS OF THEIR SEPARATE PERILOUS ADVENTURES...

IT'S ALMOST AS IF THE *PLANET ITSELF* IS OUT TO *DESTROY* US!

IT'S UNCANNY! WE'D BETTER GET OUT OF HERE--HEAD BACK TO EARTH RIGHT NOW WHILE WE CAN! WE CAN'T KEEP BATTLING A *PHANTOM ENEMY*!

12

BUT, INCREDIBLY, BEFORE THE INTREPID DUO CAN TAKE OFF, THE PLANET ITSELF CONVULSES INTO FURIOUS ACTION...

Uhh MOUNTAIN PEAKS HAVE BECOME HANDS REACHING OUT TO SEIZE US... WITH TERRIBLE STRENGTH!

FIGHT, *GREEN LANTERN!* DON'T GIVE UP! WE'LL FIND A WAY TO GET OUT OF THIS!

AHRRRR!

SUITING HIS ACTIONS TO HIS WORDS, *FLASH* VIBRATES HIM-SELF AT A FANTASTIC RATE...

TRYING TO HOLD ME WHEN I'M VIBRATING LIKE THIS MUST BE LIKE TRYING TO HOLD A LIGHTNING BOLT!

AND *GREEN LANTERN*, TOO, REVEALS HIS TRUE METTLE IN THE CRISIS...

MY GREEN BEAM HAS CREATED A GIANT *RIVETING MACHINE* SO POWERFUL THAT EVEN THE MOUNTAIN CAN'T WITHSTAND IT! IT'S DROPPING ME LIKE A HOT POTATO!

13

AND SOON, THE TWO VICTORS OVER THE STRANGE PLANET FLY HOMEWARD VIA *GREEN LANTERN'S* POWER BEAM...

...AND WE MAY *NEVER* SOLVE THE PUZZLE OF *WHY* YOU WERE SEIZED BY THAT SPACESHIP, *FLASH!* OR THE MEANING OF ALL THE THINGS THAT HAPPENED TO US BACK THERE!

TRUE...

EDITOR'S NOTE: IN ORDER TO *STAND* IN THE *GREEN* BUBBLE, FLASH HAS REMOVED HIS *YELLOW* BOOTS!

THERE DOESN'T SEEM TO BE ANY *RHYME* OR *REASON* BEHIND THE ATTACKS ON US! BUT RIGHT NOW IT STRIKES ME THAT WE'D BETTER HUSTLE HOME AGAIN TO OUR WEEK-END PARTY--AS *HAL JORDAN* AND *BARRY ALLEN*, OF COURSE!

IRIS HATES TO BE KEPT WAITING!

I IMAGINE CAROL ISN'T TOO HAPPY ABOUT OUR DISAPPEARANCE EITHER! WE'LL HAVE TO EXPLAIN IT SOMEHOW...

THEN, BACK ON EARTH...

GREEN LANTERN, LOOK--!

GREAT GUARDIANS!? IS IT POSSIBLE--!?

14

149

RETURNING FROM THE **PLANET OF MYSTERY** IN FAR-OFF SPACE, THE TWO SUPER-HEROES ARE ASTONISHED TO DISCOVER THAT THE EARTH HAS CHANGED INCREDIBLY DURING THEIR BRIEF ABSENCE!

I DON'T KNOW, **GL**! BUT I MAKE A MOTION THE FIRST THING WE DO IS TACKLE THAT HUGE ROBOT!

SECONDED, **FLASH**! LET'S GO!

THAT GIGANTIC ROBOT-- STANDING ON GUARD THERE-- AS IF IT'S **KEEPING WATCH** FOR SOME REASON **OVER THE CITY**!

AND THE PEOPLE-- THEIR FACES--GRIM LIKE **PRISONERS**! WHAT IN THE WORLD IS GOING ON HERE, **FLASH**?

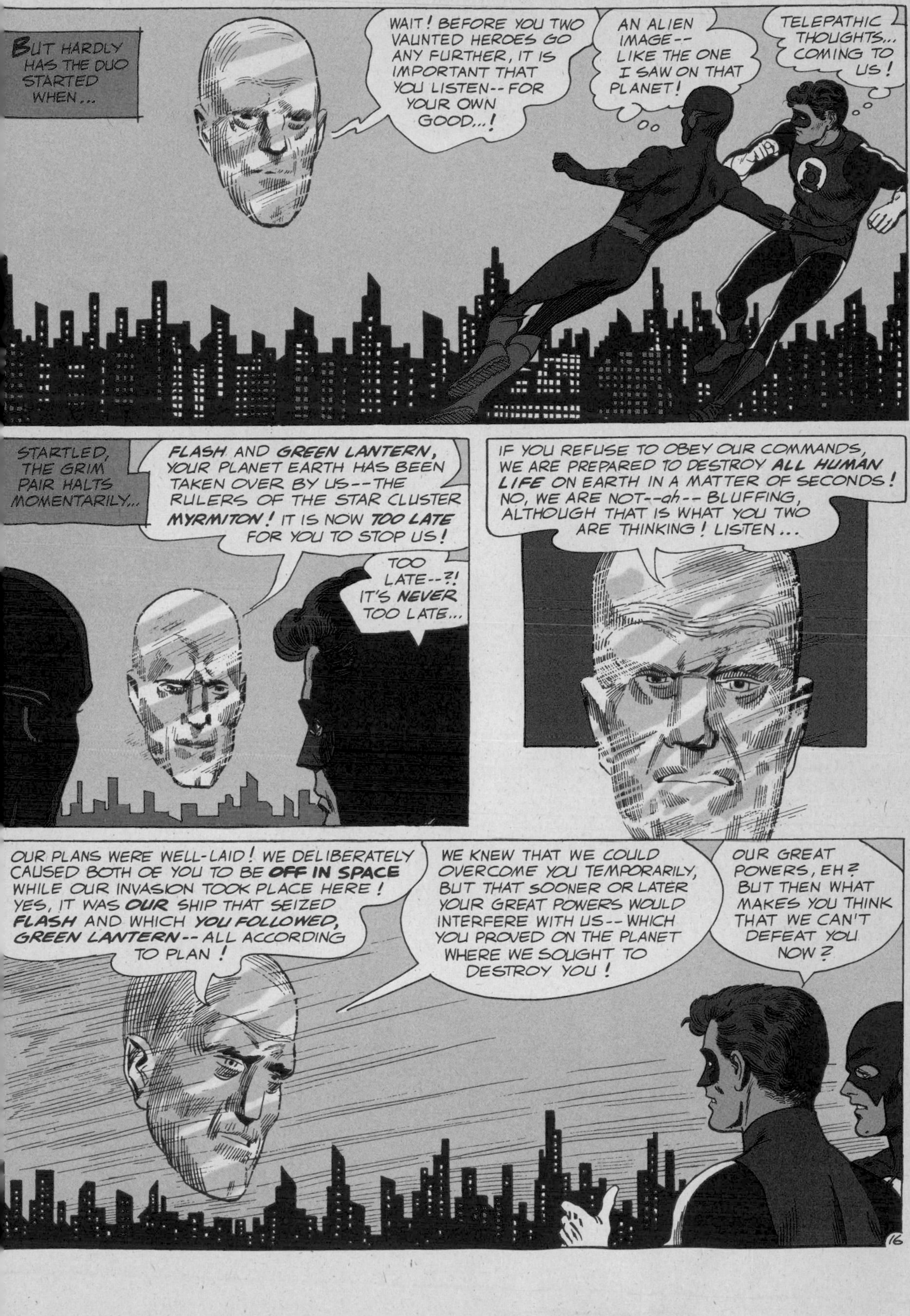
BUT HARDLY HAS THE DUO STARTED WHEN...
WAIT! BEFORE YOU TWO VAUNTED HEROES GO ANY FURTHER, IT IS IMPORTANT THAT YOU LISTEN-- FOR YOUR OWN GOOD...!
AN ALIEN IMAGE-- LIKE THE ONE I SAW ON THAT PLANET!
TELEPATHIC THOUGHTS... COMING TO US!
STARTLED, THE GRIM PAIR HALTS MOMENTARILY...
FLASH AND GREEN LANTERN, YOUR PLANET EARTH HAS BEEN TAKEN OVER BY US--THE RULERS OF THE STAR CLUSTER MYRMITON! IT IS NOW TOO LATE FOR YOU TO STOP US!
TOO LATE--?! IT'S NEVER TOO LATE...
IF YOU REFUSE TO OBEY OUR COMMANDS, WE ARE PREPARED TO DESTROY ALL HUMAN LIFE ON EARTH IN A MATTER OF SECONDS! NO, WE ARE NOT--ah-- BLUFFING, ALTHOUGH THAT IS WHAT YOU TWO ARE THINKING! LISTEN...
OUR PLANS WERE WELL-LAID! WE DELIBERATELY CAUSED BOTH OF YOU TO BE OFF IN SPACE WHILE OUR INVASION TOOK PLACE HERE! YES, IT WAS OUR SHIP THAT SEIZED FLASH AND WHICH YOU FOLLOWED, GREEN LANTERN-- ALL ACCORDING TO PLAN!
WE KNEW THAT WE COULD OVERCOME YOU TEMPORARILY, BUT THAT SOONER OR LATER YOUR GREAT POWERS WOULD INTERFERE WITH US-- WHICH YOU PROVED ON THE PLANET WHERE WE SOUGHT TO DESTROY YOU!
OUR GREAT POWERS, EH? BUT THEN WHAT MAKES YOU THINK THAT WE CAN'T DEFEAT YOU NOW?
16

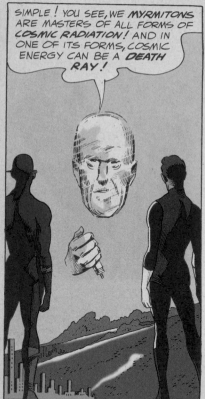

SIMPLE! YOU SEE, WE *MYRMITONS* ARE MASTERS OF ALL FORMS OF *COSMIC RADIATION!* AND IN ONE OF ITS FORMS, COSMIC ENERGY CAN BE A *DEATH RAY!*

EVEN AT THIS MOMENT IF I PRESSED THE GADGET I AM HOLDING -- *OR* IF ANYTHING HAPPENED TO ME -- A FLOOD-TIDE OF COSMIC ANNIHILATION WOULD ENGULF YOUR ENTIRE PLANET! I ADVISE YOU *NOT* TO TAKE THE RISK...

YOU MUST SURRENDER AT ONCE...

WE'LL FIND A WAY OUT OF THIS SOMEHOW.. BUT MEANWHILE WE HAVE TO SURRENDER! WE HAVE *NO CHOICE!*

AND SECONDS LATER, AFTER THE BITTER PAIR HAS GRIMLY ANNOUNCED ITS CAPITULATION...

GOOD! YOU ARE VERY WISE! THIS IS WHAT YOU MUST DO! *GREEN LANTERN,* TAKE OFF YOUR *POWER RING* -- AND TOSS IT *INTO THE YELLOW BEAM* NOW COVERING YOU! AS FOR YOU, *FLASH!*

A *SPECIAL RADIATION* WILL BE DIRECTED AT YOU WHICH WILL COMPLETELY REMOVE FROM YOU ANY TRACE OF YOUR AMAZING *SUPER-SPEED!* I WARN YOU -- ANY ATTEMPT TO AVOID YOUR FATE WILL CAUSE YOUR EARTH TO BE DESTROYED!

MOMENTS LATER, RELUCTANTLY...

THERE GOES MY RING! I HAD TO DO IT! I COULDN'T RISK THE LIVES OF BILLIONS!

MY *SUPER-SPEED* GONE!

17

SOON, TWO FORLORN FIGURES STRIDE THROUGH THE CITY...

WHAT ARE WE GOING TO DO, *FLASH?* HOW CAN WE DEFEAT THESE *MYRMITONS?* IT WAS A CLEVER STROKE OF THEM TO GET US OFF THE PLANET WHILE THEY SUBDUED EARTH--

--AND THEN TO DEPRIVE US OF OUR *SPECIAL POWERS!* BUT I'M STILL *GREEN LANTERN* AND YOU'RE STILL *THE FLASH!* THERE MUST BE *SOMETHING* WE CAN DO!

AS GLOOM TINGES THE INDOMITABLE FEATURES OF THE *EMERALD GLADIATOR...*

FLASH WON'T EVEN TALK TO ME! HE SEEMS TO HAVE LOST THE FIERY SPIRIT THAT ALWAYS SHONE OUT IN ANY SITUATION! BUT--IT'S EASY TO UNDERSTAND...

IT'S HARD TO LIVE UNDER THE *HEEL OF A CONQUEROR!* THE *MYRMITONS* HAVE EVEN FORBIDDEN THE USE OF ALL VEHICLES -- BECAUSE THEY COULD BE USED TO ATTACK THE INVADERS! AND ONLY THE *MYRMITONS* THEMSELVES ARE ALLOWED...

...TO RIDE THROUGH THE CITY! LIKE THAT CAR FULL OF THEM THAT IS ALMOST MOWING DOWN THESE PEDESTRIANS! A SIGHT LIKE THAT COULD MAKE *ANYONE* GRIM AND SILENT!

SO *GREEN LANTERN* THINKS I'VE LOST MY SPIRIT...!

18

Then... **GREEN LANTERN, PRETEND YOU DON'T HEAR ME! JUST KEEP LOOKING STRAIGHT AHEAD-- THAT'S IT!**

THE FLASH-- COMMUNICATING WITH ME MENTALLY!? BUT HOW--?!

I'LL EXPLAIN! HEAD FOR THAT PARK BENCH! NO DOUBT THEY'RE WATCHING US--AND IT WILL LOOK AS IF WE'RE MERELY RESTING!

SOON, TO GREEN LANTERN'S ASTONISHMENT HE FINDS THAT HE AND FLASH ARE CONVERSING BY TELEPATHY!

...AND THEN WHEN WE WERE STANDING THERE BEFORE THE MYRMITON IMAGE A WHILE AGO, I SUDDENLY THOUGHT OF A WAY TO OUTWIT OUR FOES! HERE'S WHAT I DID... THERE WAS ONLY A SECOND OR LESS IN WHICH TO ACT...

"I NEVER MOVED SO FAST IN MY LIFE! NEITHER YOU NOR THE MYRMITONS REALIZED I WAS ON MY WAY..."

I'VE GOT TO GET...

...INTO THE DEPARTMENT STORE...

...WHERE GL AND I SAW THAT TABLEAU OF THE TWO OF US...!

Editor's Note:

FOR A BRIEF MOMENT THE IMAGE OF FLASH LINGERS IN THE PLACE HE HAS JUST VACATED! BUT THIS MOMENT IS ENOUGH FOR THE INCREDIBLE SPEEDSTER TO CARRY OUT A DARING SCHEME!

"SOON, IN THE MEREST SPLIT- INSTANT..."

A GOOD THING I NOTICED THE "POWER RING" ON THIS DUMMY FIGURE OF GREEN LANTERN! WITHOUT IT MY PLAN WOULD BE IMPOSSIBLE!

"IT TOOK ME ALMOST NO TIME TO RETURN! BY THEN I WAS REALLY MOVING..."

I'M TAKING GREEN LANTERN'S RING OFF-- AND REPLACING IT WITH THE FALSE REPLICA-- SO QUICKLY THAT HE DOESN'T REALIZE ANYTHING IS HAPPENING!

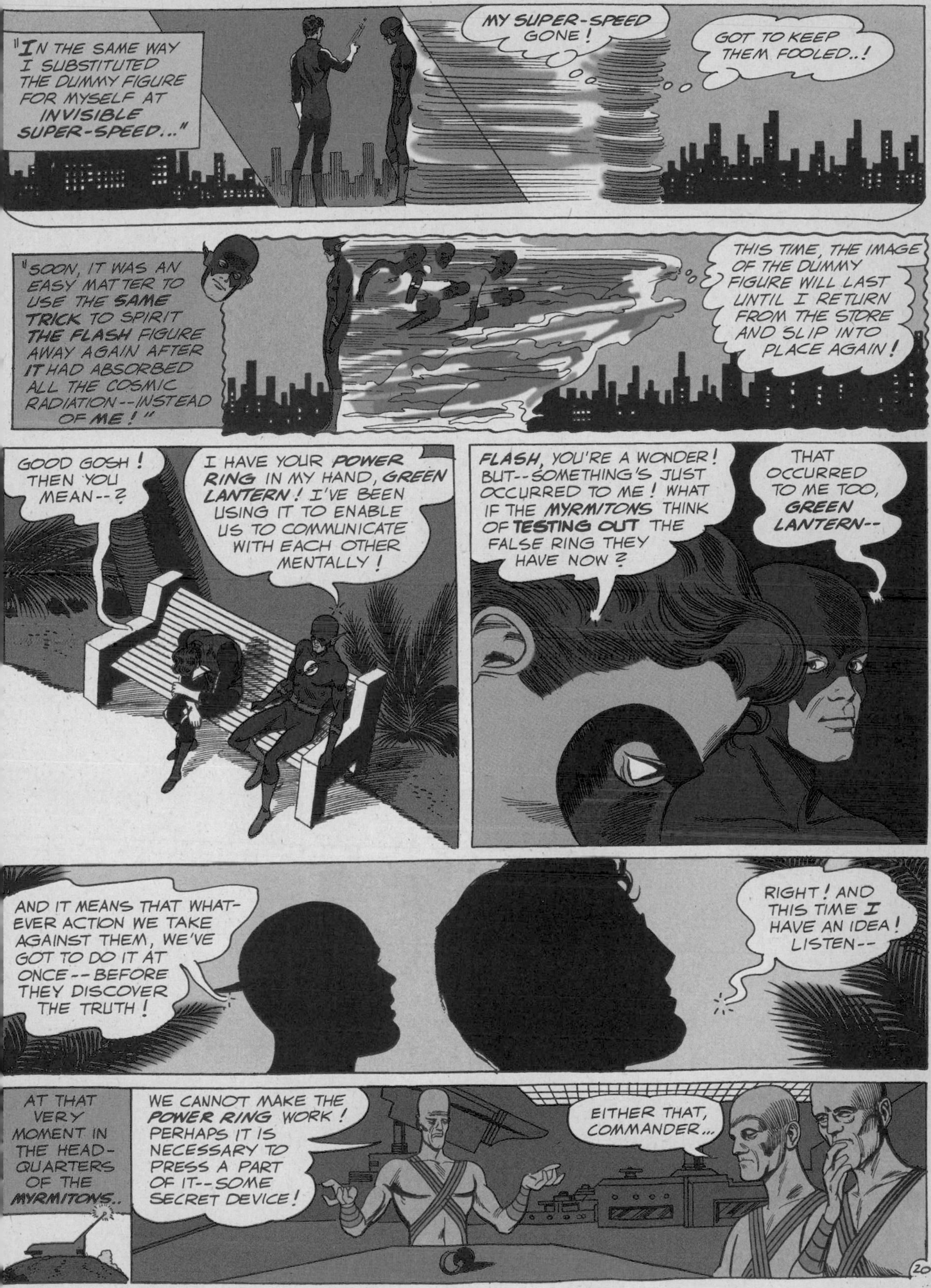
"IN THE SAME WAY I SUBSTITUTED THE DUMMY FIGURE FOR MYSELF AT INVISIBLE SUPER-SPEED..."
MY SUPER-SPEED GONE!
GOT TO KEEP THEM FOOLED..!
"SOON, IT WAS AN EASY MATTER TO USE THE SAME TRICK TO SPIRIT THE FLASH FIGURE AWAY AGAIN AFTER IT HAD ABSORBED ALL THE COSMIC RADIATION--INSTEAD OF ME!"
THIS TIME, THE IMAGE OF THE DUMMY FIGURE WILL LAST UNTIL I RETURN FROM THE STORE AND SLIP INTO PLACE AGAIN!
GOOD GOSH! THEN YOU MEAN--?
I HAVE YOUR POWER RING IN MY HAND, GREEN LANTERN! I'VE BEEN USING IT TO ENABLE US TO COMMUNICATE WITH EACH OTHER MENTALLY!
FLASH, YOU'RE A WONDER! BUT--SOMETHING'S JUST OCCURRED TO ME! WHAT IF THE MYRMITONS THINK OF TESTING OUT THE FALSE RING THEY HAVE NOW?
THAT OCCURRED TO ME TOO, GREEN LANTERN--
AND IT MEANS THAT WHATEVER ACTION WE TAKE AGAINST THEM, WE'VE GOT TO DO IT AT ONCE--BEFORE THEY DISCOVER THE TRUTH!
RIGHT! AND THIS TIME I HAVE AN IDEA! LISTEN--
AT THAT VERY MOMENT IN THE HEADQUARTERS OF THE MYRMITONS..
WE CANNOT MAKE THE POWER RING WORK! PERHAPS IT IS NECESSARY TO PRESS A PART OF IT--SOME SECRET DEVICE!
EITHER THAT, COMMANDER...
20

...OR WE HAVE BEEN TRICKED SOMEHOW-- AND THAT IS **NOT** GREEN LANTERN'S **REAL** POWER RING!

BY THE **SEVEN SUNS** OF **MYRMITON!** YOU MAY BE RIGHT, MPONOS!

AND IF THAT IS SO, **GREEN LANTERN** ALONG WITH **FLASH**-- WHO MAY IN SOME WAY HAVE **ALSO** DECEIVED US-- COULD EVEN NOW BE PREPARING TO **ATTACK!** WE MUST SEEK THEM OUT-- DESTROY THEM!

WAIT...

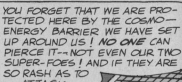

YOU FORGET THAT WE ARE PROTECTED HERE BY THE COSMO--ENERGY BARRIER WE HAVE SET UP AROUND US! **NO ONE** CAN PIERCE IT--NOT EVEN OUR TWO SUPER-FOES! AND IF THEY ARE SO RASH AS TO ATTACK--

COMMANDER LOOK--!

FLASH AND **GREEN LANTERN**--COMING AT US!

THEN OUR FEARS WERE JUSTIFIED--

--THEY FOOLED US!!

NO--IT IS THEY WHO ARE THE FOOLS, MPONOS! THEY CANNOT POSSIBLY BREAK THROUGH OUR ENERGY BARRIER! AND THE MOMENT THEY ARE STOPPED BY IT--

--THEY WILL BECOME PERFECT TARGETS! AT THIS DISTANCE A **COSMO-BLASTER** CANNOT MISS!

21

AND THE NEXT MOMENT INCREDIBLY--

THE BARRIER STOPPED THEM COLD!

AND NOW THEY ARE STOPPED FOREVER BY OUR *COSMO-BLAST!*

BUT IS IT REALLY TRUE THAT BOTH *GREEN LANTERN* AND *THE FLASH* HAVE BEEN DE-FEATED--DESTROYED--AT ONE TERRIBLE STROKE? IT WOULD SEEM SO, AND YET TO UNDER-STAND WHAT UNDER-LIES MERE APPEAR-ANCES, LET US TURN BACK TEMPORARILY...

...TO THE MOMENT WHEN THE *GREEN-GARBED CRUSADER* WAS DESCRIBING HIS PLAN TO *THE FLASH*...

...AND EARLIER WHEN WE WERE FACING THE *MYRMITONS,* MY RING REVEALED THE PRESENCE OF AN *INVISIBLE FORCE-FIELD* AROUND THEIR HEADQUARTERS! AT THE VERY LEAST IT WOULD SLOW US DOWN IF WE ATTACKED DIRECTLY! SO--

...MY IDEA IS THIS! WHY DON'T WE *PRETEND* WE'RE ATTACKING--BUT INSTEAD USE MY RING TO POWER OUR TWO DUMMY FIGURES FROM THE STORE! THAT STUNT WILL DISTRACT THE *MYRMITONS* LONG ENOUGH...

...FOR THE TWO OF US SECRETLY TO REACH OUR FOES VIA A TUNNEL BORED UNDER THEIR HEADQUARTERS WHERE THE *FORCE-FIELD* DOESN'T EXIST!

NOW, *YOU'RE* THE WONDER, *GL!* LET'S CARRY OUT YOUR PLAN!

AND THUS MOST UNEXPECTEDLY FOR THE INVADERS, WHO HAVE THOUGHT *FLASH* AND *GREEN LANTERN* OUT OF ACTION...

THAT'S IT, *FLASH!* HIT THEM HARD-- AND KEEP HITTING! WE MUSTN'T GIVE THEM A CHANCE!

NO! IT IS NOT POSSIBLE--!

A MOMENT LATER WHILE THE *SCARLET SPEEDSTER* RENDERS USELESS ALL THE EQUIPMENT IN SIGHT, MOVING AT A FANTASTIC RATE...

I DON'T KNOW WHICH OF THE MACHINES HERE PRODUCES THE *COSMIC DEATH RAY,* SO JUST TO BE ON THE SAFE SIDE I'LL TAKE THEM ALL APART AT *SUPER-SPEED!*

..*GREEN LANTERN'S* MIGHTY *POWER BEAM* FLARES OUT TO FREEZE HIS FOES IN PLACE!

...AND NOW LISTEN TO THE CONDITIONS WHICH YOU *MYRMITONS* MUST FOLLOW, IF YOU WISH TO ESCAPE FROM EARTH WITH YOUR LIVES!

WE--WE ACCEPT YOUR CONDITIONS, *GREEN LANTERN*-- WHATEVER THEY ARE!

LATER THAT DAY, AS THE INVADING SPACESHIPS LEAVE EARTH...

GREEN LANTERN AND I HAD THIS ALL PLANNED AHEAD OF TIME! WE'RE HOLDING A CERTAIN NUMBER OF THE MYRMITONS AS HOSTAGES-- TO MAKE SURE THAT THE OTHERS NEVER AGAIN ATTEMPT TO INVADE EARTH!

LATER, IF CONDITIONS WARRANT IT, WE MAY ALLOW THE HOSTAGES TO RETURN HOME TOO! WE MAY..!

AS AN EXHILARATING SENSE OF FREEDOM SPREADS OVER THE LAND...

HURRAY! THE LAST OF THE ALIENS HAVE GONE! EARTH IS OURS AGAIN!

WE'VE GOT TO INTERVIEW GREEN LANTERN AND FLASH--

eh? THAT'S ODD! FLASH AND GREEN LANTERN WERE HERE A MINUTE AGO! BUT NOW WHERE ARE THEY? EVERYONE IS WAITING TO LEARN ALL THE DETAILS OF HOW THEY DEFEATED THE MYRMITONS--

WELL, HOW DO YOU LIKE THAT? WITH THE WHOLE WORLD CLAMORING TO SEE AND HEAR FLASH AND GREEN LANTERN ON TELEVISION--THEY DISAPPEAR!

AT THAT MOMENT...

WE'VE GOT TO HUSTLE, HAL!

I'M WITH YOU, BARRY! BUT WHAT WILL WE TELL THE GIRLS? WE CAN'T LET THEM SUSPECT...

AFTER A QUICK HUDDLE...

THERE THEY ARE NOW!

BARRY AND HAL!?

24

159

THEN YOU TWO WERE *CAPTURED* BY THE *MYRMITONS*!

THAT'S RIGHT, CAROL!

IN A WAY AT LEAST, IT'S TRUE!

BUT THANKS TO--er-- *GREEN LANTERN* AND *FLASH*, HERE WE ARE SAFE AND SOUND!

AND THAT'S JUST ABOUT THE *EXACT TRUTH* TOO!

LATER, WHEN A BELATED ARCHERY MATCH FINALLY GETS UNDER WAY...

I CAN'T UNDERSTAND IT! BARRY AND HAL WERE SO ANXIOUS TO PROVE WHICH WAS THE BETTER ARCHER--BUT NOW ALL THEIR ARROWS ARE MISSING THE TARGET!

CAN'T CALL EITHER OF US THE WINNER, HAL! I GUESS OUR *SPORTS* CONTEST HAS ENDED IN A *TIE*!

SUITS ME, BARRY!

I DON'T GET IT! IT'S AS IF THEY SUDDENLY BECAME SO FRIENDLY TOWARD EACH OTHER THAT EACH WAS TRYING TO *LET THE OTHER WIN*!

ANOTHER ADVENTURE STARRING THE DYNAMIC DUO--*FLASH* AND *GREEN LANTERN*--WILL APPEAR SOON! WATCH FOR IT!

The End

25